KINGDOM GROWTH THROUGH MISSIONAL BEHAVIOR

—*Growing a Relational Congregation*

Hollis L. Green & E. Basil Jackson

KINGDOM GROWTH THOUGH MISSIONAL BEHAVIOR
—*Growing a Relational Congregation*

Copyright © 2019 by Hollis L. Green

Library of Congress Control Number: 2019905122

Green, Hollis L., 1933 –

ISBN 978-1-935434-91-7

Subject Codes and Description: 1: SOC039000 Social Science: Sociology And Religion 2: REL077000 Religion: Faith 3: REL 006100 Religion: Biblical Criticism & Interpretation –New Testament.

All rights reserved, including the right to reproduce this book or any part thereof in any form, except for inclusion of brief quotations in a review, without the written permission of GlobalEdAdvance PRESS and the author. Old Testament scriptures not otherwise noted are from the NIV. New Testament scriptures not otherwise noted are from the KJV.

Cover by GlobalGraphics

Printed in Australia, Brazil, France, Germany, Italy, Poland, Russia, Spain, EU, UK and (3 sites) USA and available on the Espresso Book Machine©. Order books from www/gea-books.com/bookstore/ or any place good books are sold.

The Press does not have ownership of the contents of a book; this is the author's work and the author owns the copyright. All theory, concepts, constructs, and perspectives are those of the author and not necessarily the Press. They are presented for open and free discussion of the issues involved. All comments and feedback should be directed to the Email: [comments4author@aol.com] and the comments will be forwarded to the author for response.

Published by

GreenWine Family Books™

A division of GlobalEdAdvancePress

www.gea-books.com

DEDICATION

This work is dedicated with affection to

Maranatha Bible Church,
Converse, Texas, USA

To congratulate a band of believers
On three decades of ministry
With a missional lifestyle and
A desire for global expansion of the
Kingdom of God through the care and
Education of believers.

Founder Dr. Rander E. Draper, Sr. and wife, Darlene, have led a growing congregation in a global missional lifestyle ministry for thirty years. Preaching, teaching or singing, the Drapers always honor the Word of God whether at home or on global mission fields. Global Educational Advance PRESS wishes to congratulate them on their faithful congregational growth, development, perpetual care and education of souls through their missional ministry. We are pleased to be friends of this ministry couple, their family, the growing congregation and expanding global activity.

Contents

Foreword: *Maranatha Bible Church*   11

Prologue: *Spiritual Adoption and Surrogate Nurturing*   15

Introduction: *Foundational Stones for a New Congregation*   21

1. **EXTEND Witnessing Through Missional Behavior**   27
   — *adopting the thinking, behaviors, and practices of a missionary in order to globalize the gospel.*

2. **AMPLIFY Worship Through Celebration**   39
   — *a vertical experience that recognizes the "worth-ship" of God.*

3. **EXPAND Fellowship By Congregational Activity**   59
   — *a gathering of kinship groups and friends with common interest and values for fellowship.*

4. **MATURE Constituency Through Open-Door Study Classes**   77
   — *making biblical discipleship a core learning experience together with relevant textbook studies to equip community and church families to become problem-solvers and effective servant leaders.*

5. **INCREASE The Care Of Souls In Cells**   91
   — *maturing believers in small groups invested with the cure/care of souls through faith, spiritual nourishment, friendship, and fellowship.*

6. **EDUCATE Community And Churchgoers Through A Learning Centre Ministry**   105
   — *a moral and intellectual effort to equip believers to become problem-solvers and effective servant leaders to advance the gospel.*

7. **AUGMENT Outreach By A Nonsectarian Worldview And Extend Evangelism Through Missionary Support**   135
   — *a value added asset to enable believers to participate in global outreach through personal and financial support.*

8	GROW Constituency By Multiplying Congregations	155

— reaching local people to form new fellowship and interest groups that become new congregations.

9	ADVANCE The Kingdom By Planting Churches	167

— establishing teaching/learning centers and mission stations that develop into places of worship.

10	DEVELOP Quality By Assessing Strengths And Weaknesses	197

— quantifying orthodoxy and orthopraxis by comparing the local congregation with the seven sample churches of Revelation

11	IMPROVE Evangelism By Associating Conversion With The Human Birth Cycle	221

— a process, not an event, that enables converts to become disciples

12	ENHANCE Believers Discipleship Training Using Knowledge Of Human Development	251

– education that reflects generic New Testament values and faith-based lifestyles

Afterword		287
About the Authors		289
Appendix A	Other Books	293
Appendix B	Compare Your Church with the Seven Churches Strengths and Weaknesses Assessment	298
Appendix C	Academic Primary/Secondary Age-level Divisions	301
Appendix D	Guidance for Caretakers, Mentors, and coaches	303
Appendix E	Guidance for New Converts	314
Appendix F	How and Why Pristine Congregations Grew	317
Bibliography		328

Kingdom Growth Through Missional Behavior

—Growing a Relational Congregation

Kingdom Growth through Missional Behavior is adopting the thinking, behaviors, and practices of a missionary in order to establish and globalize the message of Grace.

Foreword

Maranatha Bible Church
Converse, TX

Love Deeper than a Song

After much prayer and being led by the Spirit, God impressed upon the heart of Rander E. Draper, Sr. a desire to plant a Bible teaching church in Northeast San Antonio. In 1988 Pastor Draper shared his vision, purpose and mission for the birth of Maranatha — a Body of Believers to bring glory to God through worship and praise.

- We are committed to assembling together for fellowship and participation in the ordinances of Baptism and the Lord's Supper.
- We are a mission-minded church, dedicated to winning souls for Christ and equipping the saints for the work of ministry.
- We strive to strengthen the family unit and to be a haven of love, encouragement and acceptance for all peoples.
- We are committed to building up the Body of Christ through the ministry of prayer.
- We are committed to being a Bible teaching church where the Word of God is the final authority in life and decisions.

The Lord gives many gifts to His people and greatest of these is love. Thankfully, Pastor Draper possesses and dispenses love by heaping handfuls. You need only to hear him sing about his first love to know how much he loves Jesus…and can he sing! But his love goes deeper than a song. It rolls up its sleeves and goes to work to make sure that people not only have their spiritual needs met, but their physical, material, family needs met as well.

Just as his parents gave him a good foundation, Pastor Draper has given Maranatha Bible Church in Converse, Texas, a good foundation through sound doctrine. He clearly states, **"Sound doctrine is everything because it restrains sin and the work of Satan. It breaks the spirit of confusion; it stabilizes, strengthens, matures, and liberates the saints from bondage."** His love and spiritual guidance has brought us through three decades of growth and ministry. His heart is in missions and a missional lifestyle for believers. We are pleased that even the name of our church "Maranatha" means *"The Lord is Coming!"* The Hope of Lord's Return and the desire to see Jesus causes believers to anticipate the Glory of His Coming and to live a life that pleases Him. (1 John 3:1-3)

2018 was filled with celebration and reflection on God's faithfulness during the past three decades. We kicked off the year by hosing the January Baptist Minister's Union City Wide Institute with congregants from throughout the city. In February, the pastor and Darlene, took a small team to Uganda and Rwanda, to share the Gospel with hundreds of East Africans. In March we conducted a Bible Conference with Gideon

Levytam, founder of Holy Scriptures of Israel Bible Society. In April, Maranatha members and friends traveled to Israel to visit the Holy Land sites. During the Anniversary Celebration Gala in May we were blessed with many programs and visitors from the USA and around the world. During the summer months Maranatha Youth took leadership for worship, Sunday school, and traveling. The youth went to MoRanch in the hill country for a Spirit-filled summer camping experience. In October, Maranatha celebrated the Institution of Marriage with a Wedding Vow Renewal Ceremony where 18 couples committed to a covenant relationship. In November we honored those who served our nation in a Military Appreciation Day Celebration. December concluded the THIRTY YEAR ANNIVERSARY by celebrating the birth of Jesus during the annual Christmas Program which included Baptisms, the Lord's Supper and ended the yearlong celebration with a joyful New Year's Eve Celebration, featuring various choirs, visiting churches, and preaching of the Word of God. Through the year we focused on giving thanks to the Lord for three decades of ministry.

—The Family of Believers at ***Maranatha Bible Church.***

> *"He is no fool*
> *who gives up what he cannot keep*
> *to gain what he cannot lose."* —Jim Elliot

One of five US missionaries martyred (1956) while taking the Gospel to the Huaorani people in the rain forest of Ecuador.

∼

Where are their replacements or successors? You may sign up at the altar in your place of worship! Ask God for guidance on a missional lifestyle and be willing to follow the leadership of the Spirit.

Prologue

Spiritual Adoption and Surrogate Nurturing

Hollis L. Green

When my father passed in 1937, I lacked three months being five (5) years old. My mother was left with three small children: a girl 9, myself, and a baby just 6 months old. Mother sang in the choir and taught an adult Bible Class. Her concern "What am I to do with a growing boy during church?" On the first Sunday following my father's passing, mother took us all to church. Two men, Ira Johnson and Lester Johnson, no relation but they shared a common interest in children, both came to mother that first Sunday and asked, "Mrs. Green, if you don't mind we will take charge of Hollis during the service?" Mother's prayers were answered, and she could teach the class and sing in the choir without concerns as to the mischief her son might create.

Ira and Lester instructed me where to sit and to go to the bathroom and get a drink of water before the service began. I was not to move from that spot until the final "Amen!" Usually, one of the men sat behind me on the second seat and I sat on the first pew at the end. I was instructed to pay attention, listen to the songs and the sermon. The pew had a nice curved end and I learned to prop my arm on the end piece and put my hand under my chin and take a nap looking straight at the pulpit. At least I was quiet.

Through the years I became interested in what the pastor was saying about God and Jesus and other stuff. I remember learning that God was my Father and that Jesus was my big Brother. At age 9, I was elected President of my Sunday school class (ages 9-11) and became serious about bible study. We had a teacher who was not always present, and when he did not show I would just teach the lesson. You see, my mother was a school teacher, and required my older sister and me to begin studying the lesson Sunday afternoon for the next Sunday. By Wednesday she would ask one of us to teach the lesson to the family. Mother wanted her children to be informed participants in class. This is why at age 12, the class elected me as their teacher. Thank God for a teaching mother and for Ira and Lester Johnson who took an interest and exercised a "spiritual adoption" to do basic watch care for me at church.

When I was 12, the pastor announced a special meeting for tithe paying male members. I went. As soon as the pastor arrived, he thought it not good that I was there because they were to discuss behavioral matters about two church leaders. The Johnson men stood, *"This young man will be a church leader someday and he should learn both sides of the situation."* Then several others asked for me to stay. Perhaps I was too young to hear about *hanky-panky* between the music director and the piano player, but I thought it was some kind of non-church music. Anyway, the men standing up for me taught me a worthy lesson. Yes, I learned something about the other side of the coin. Later, when I learned that *hanky-panky* was dubious behavior of a sexual nature and considered improper by the church, I learned a good lesson for my future.

At age 14, I was asked to speak on a Wednesday night at a small rural church. The next Sunday evening my pastor developed a sore throat and asked me to speak. After the service, Lester Johnson came to mother, *"Mrs. Green, if it is OK with you, Ira and I would like to buy Hollis a preaching suit."* It was my second suit and I wore it with pride and had my first studio picture taken in the Johnson suit. My first one was made from my father's best 3-piece suit in time for his funeral. Mother cut the suit, white shirt, tie and belt down to my size. Underclothes, socks and shoes were mine that I wore with the made over suit to my father's funeral.

The Church Council asked that I serve as Church Youth Leader during my last two years of high school. I initiated a Saturday evening youth service to rally the youth; we averaged about 500 on Saturday night with the young people in charge. The first week-end after graduation, I began youth revivals in Arkansas, Alabama and West Virginia. God was with me and I had Mother's Bible and the Johnson preaching suit.

My conclusion after 65 years of ministry in 106 countries: the church needs more teaching mothers and we sure need more men in the church who care for children the way Ira and Lester Johnson watched over me. In fact, their love for children was further demonstrated when, as childless married men, they adopted two sisters and each one raised one, but kept them together as sisters in church, school and in a family relationship. God bless such men who care for orphaned girls and poor little boys without a father's care. Surely, God has a special place in heaven for such people.

Faith-based groups and the world would be much better if more men had such a "father's heart" filled with the Divine Nurturing Attribute that comes with a deep and abiding spiritual relationship with God. There is a need for spiritual adoption of the young without the watch care of a father. Faith-based groups need both men and women who will serve as remedial and surrogate parents for the young and the new converts if the Kingdom is to grow!

> 25. But whosoever bows down to observe the complete prescriptive usage and the unrestrained opportunity to continue in the word and not become a forgetful hearer, but one who behaves the prescribed deeds, **this man shall by the blood be set apart for consecrated action**. 26. If any man among you seem to be devout, and restrains not his unnatural language, he deceives his own heart and his service to God is ineffective. 27. **Free from all that would dim the transparency in belief and conduct before God and the Father is this, to go see and relieve the orphans without a father's protection and the women lacking a husband in their distress, and to keep himself untainted with guilt.** (James 1:25-27 EDNT)

> 30. And you shall love the Lord your God with your whole heart ,and with your whole existence, and with all your moral understanding, and with all your ability and strength: 31. namely this, You shall love as yourself those near you. There is no other commandment greater than these. (Mark 12:30-31 EDNT)

Structure For Action And Inclusion

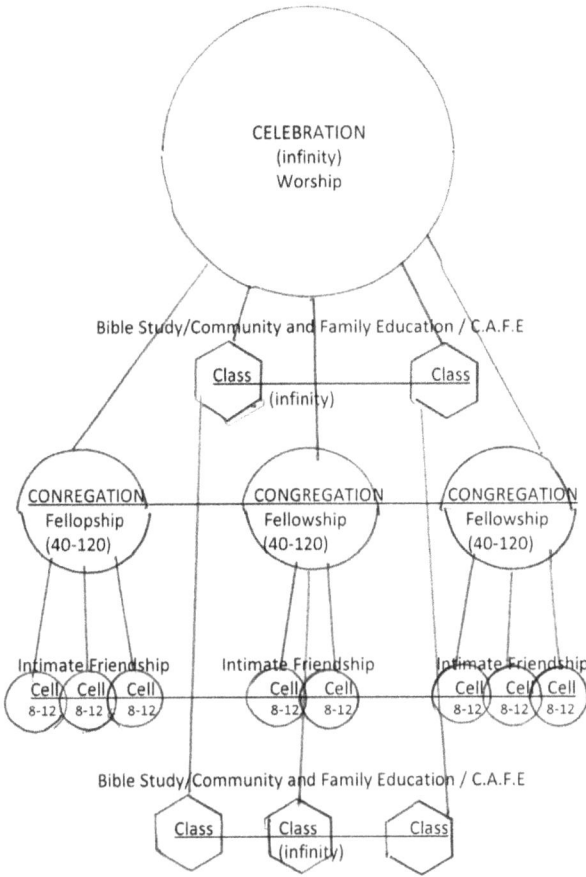

||||||||||||||||||||||||||||||||||||||||||||||||||||||
CELEBRATION (infinity) Worship
CONGREGATION (40-120) Fellowship
Cell (8-12) Intimate Friendship [evangelism/spiritual growth]
<u>**Class** (infinity) Bible Study/Community and Family Education / C.A.F.E.</u>

> Missional behavior is working together with God in advancing the message of redemptive grace to the world.

Introduction

Foundational Stones for a New Congregation

Based on Paul's Message to the Thessalonians

The scriptural foundation stones for this work were found in Paul's first letters to a new congregation. Paul wrote to the Thessalonians from Corinth around AD 50-51. The church was planted the year before by a short stay missionary team. The Jews of Thessalonica rejected Paul's ministry during three Sabbaths in the synagogue; as a result, the team moved to the city where the Gentiles heard the good news gladly. A pristine congregation was planted that was unspoiled, a gathering of believers who *belonged to the Lord*. While on his way to Corinth, Paul sent Timothy back to check on the condition and growth of the new believers.

When Timothy's report came that the converts were doing well but had some misconceptions regarding the Second Coming of Christ, Paul was concerned. The connection of Paul and his ministry team with the Thessalonians was deep and abiding. Timothy's report was a check on the quality of relationship, fellowship, teaching, and worship. The foundation stones for this congregation were truly relational; they were connected firmly to God, each other, and the ministry team who brought them the message of grace and redemption.

Oldest Preserved Work of Paul

Thessalonians is the oldest preserved written work of Paul. It is this writer's judgment that Paul's writing of Thessalonians was one message in two parts. The content of both parts was parallel and based on Timothy's Report. Paul encouraged believers to be steadfast in persecution and specifically described events preceding the *Parousia*. He illustrated the stability of the believer's life and encouraged converts to reject worldliness and live by moral principles. Paul dealt with their misunderstandings and reviewed both the relational conduct of the team and the content of the preaching/teaching during their short stay in Thessalonica. It appears Paul believed a knowledge of the imminent return of Jesus was essential to the spiritual foundation and function of the assembled body of believers and their missional behavior. This pristine work of Paul becomes a pattern for church planting, reaching converts, conversion follow-up, and discipleship making of young believers. Note the words of Jesus in the Gospel of John:

> 15. *I no longer call you (servants) or bond-slaves; because a bond-slave does not know what his Lord does:* **but you I have called friends; for all things that I have heard of my Father I have made known to you.** *16. You have not chosen me, but I have chosen you, and* **appointed you to go out and bring in fruit, and that your fruit should remain:** *and that <u>you should obtain answers to your prayers to make them fruitful.</u> 17. These things I command you, so that you may love one another. (John 15:15-17 EDNT)*

God's Garden

The church has been called God's Garden. What does it take to grow a garden? Diligent cultivation, careful prayerful planting, constant attention, unceasing effort and saintly patience…. then it must be touched by the Hand of God. A spiritual assembly is a growing community of believers committed to accelerating the multiplication of healthy, reproducing converts, disciple making, teaching, fellowship and worship that can grow into additional local congregations or mature into a new and established place of worship and further expand the kingdom of God. God planted a garden and placed man there to care for His handiwork. Paul called believers God's garden or field to be worked. Growing a faith-based entity is much the same as working a vegetable garden:

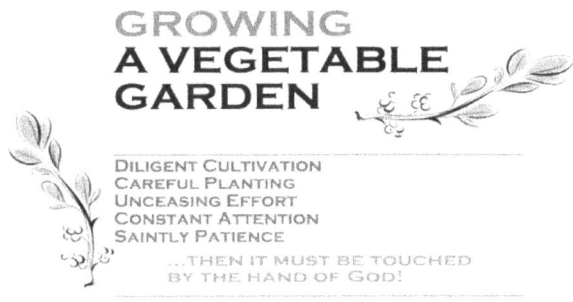

Some older folk remember the hard times when families were urged to plant vegetable gardens to supplement their food supply. Growing a garden also taught families, especially the young, that God was involved in the process, but there was plenty of work for the Gardner. I am reminded of my Grandfather's award-winning crop of corn. One Sunday a city slicker visited his church and was invited to Sunday lunch. After the meal grandfather proudly took the visitor to see his award-winning crop. The visitor thought my grandfather was too proud of his work and *declared "You should give God credit for this crop. He provided the soil, the minerals, the rain and sunshine."* Grandfather's response was simply, *"God sure left a lot for me and the boys to do!"* Oh, a city slicker is someone who knows nothing about growing corn.

Gardens were so prevalent during the war years in Great Britain that everyone still calls their back yard a garden. Now in better times they grow flowers, ground cover and shrubbery. The young and the poor have forgotten what grandparents and parents knew about gardening. Planting and growing a garden not only teaches the young and the poor the value of growing fresh vegetables; it makes them aware of God's intervention in their lives. A garden must be touched by the Hand of God regardless of the hard work of cultivating the land. Guidance in growing a garden also provides knowledge that plants are different and that they need to be organized and given special care. This knowledge may assist the poor and the unemployed through hard times; also, learning the lost art of growing a garden may become a life-saver during hard times in the future. *[and teach the wise about evangelism and church growth.]*

Planting and growing new mission stations, house churches, and teaching/learning centers that develop into new churches follows the same steps as a growing garden. Faith-based groups could use a vegetable garden as a practical and profitable teaching tool for the young.

Scriptural Study to Support this Book

(THESSALONIANS)

A study of Thessalonians would provide the reader the foundation stones for planting a faith-based congregation and a working model for growing a new congregation. A study outline of the message and the author's rendering of the *koine* Greek into a devotional language provides guidance. Planting a church is an individual process and requires the same steps as growing a garden.

Paul, Silas, and Timothy worked together to plant a new church in Thessalonica. To my knowledge, their work is the best plan to clearly understand the human effort and the spiritual dimension of church planting. I have chosen to present my rendering of Paul's writings to the Thessalonians as a starting place for any would be church planter. Study it well and remember it is not only human effort: the work must be touched by the Hand of God. Yet, the human element and labor must not be neglected.

(See CHAPTER IX for a candid rendering of I and II Thessalonians, to be used as stepping stones on the path to planting new and growing congregations.)

Kingdom Growth Through Missional Behavior

—Growing a Relational Congregation

1

EXTEND Witnessing Through Missional Behavior

— adopting the thinking, behaviors, and practices of a missionary in order to globalize the gospel.

Working Together with God

Missional living is working together with God in advancing the message of redemptive grace to the world. Wisdom brings authenticity and genuineness to the daily lives of those desiring a missional lifestyle. In Christianity, **missional living is the adoption of the attitude, thinking, behaviors, and practices of a missionary in order to engage others in the process of advancing the gospel message.** In Psalm 8: 32-35 wisdom speaks further to the faithful who attend with interest to instruction and are blessed by keeping to the proper pathway. There is a warning not to disregard the lessons learned.

Open Door of Wisdom

Those who listen and are watchful daily at the open door of wisdom will find life and favor from the Lord and will enjoy a missional reality. This is the day for fellowship among the band of believers; time for full commitment to the kingdom of God. After leaving Thessalonica, Paul journeyed to Corinth. Later he wrote the believes at Corinth about working together with God to advance the gospel. He basically told them *"God is working; you must get together."*

> *8. Now he who did the planting and the one doing the watering are part of the same process: and every man will receive a reward according to his work. 9.* **For God is working and the laborers are together:** *you are God's farm, you are God's field to be worked and God's building to be constructed. 10. According to the favor of God given to me, as a wise master builder*, **I have laid a foundation, and another will build on it. But let every worker take heed how he builds on the foundation. 11. There is no other foundation for the building but the one laid on Jesus Christ.** *(I Corinthians 3:8-11 EDNT)*

> *1.* **As we work together with God, we appeal to you not to accept the grace of God and let it go to waste.** *2. (God said, I have heard your prayers at a convenient time, and in the day of salvation I have brought you relief in a difficult situation:* **observe, now is the time for coming together; now is the day of deliverance**.*)* *(2 Corinthians 6:1-2 EDNT)*

A Distinct Lifestyle for Believers

There is a missional reality that supports a lifestyle! Essentially, a missional reality coalesces around a personalized grasp of scripture that offers a theological shift, a sociological direction, and a distinct lifestyle for believers. The missional mindset is placed in the context of viewing the Cross through the Empty Tomb, seeing culture as a vehicle of communication, the church as a force to work with not of a field in which to work, because the community and the world is a mission field ready for harvest. Sadly, the workers are few!

What is the Missionary Mindset?

What does a missionary know and how do they feel about the lost world? They know beyond a doubt they have been called to serve outside their comfort zone. They understand they must leave family and friends and travel into a strange land. They are aware of the new language and culture they will face. Called and appointed Missionaries know they must live a life worthy of financial and prayerful support from an extended constituency. They know they have limited resources and that through deputation they must raise replace funds for what is spent, or they cannot continue their work. This provides a missionary family a totally different perspective on money matters than a state side family involved in ministry. A family involved in missions cultivates a positive mindset that God is in charge of their lives and ministry. Missionaries must teach their children to live on a limited budget and that every cent saved enhances their chance of winning a soul for Christ. In fact, the missionary and their lifestyle are often lonely and full of daily difficulties. Without safe living quarters, clean sheets on the bed, good food on the table, and with only local native people protecting them against hostile forces, missionary families develop an uncertain way of life. Can we say, "*God bless the missionaries!*" Then in the next breath say, ***"Lord help me to walk the right pathway***

and demonstrate a missional lifestyle to others and be supportive of those called to serve overseas."

Hard and Harsh Work

A missionary's work is hard and often harsh, and it is even more difficult for their family. The convenience of a well-furnished home, good schools for the children, and a well-stocked food market, good transportation, and interstate highways for rapid movement are nowhere to be found in most places where missionaries life and work. Recently, by oldest son, Barton, had an opportunity to visit Guatemala for few days. He thought he was going to sing, pray and listen to missionaries speak. Traveling on a mountain road to an isolated village, to his surprise, he was handed a hammer and told **"We are building houses this week."** Another surprise, they were building on the side of a volcano (which erupted a few days later and killed many). In the past he had complained about the mile-long road up Lone Mountain to the family compound, but after this experience he sent a message, *"Tell Dad he has a wonderful road up his mountain."* It would be great if every over weight, over paid member of a faith-based congregation could spend a week on a primitive mission field as a *participator* in building rather the usual *spectator* many have become. Most likely they would return with a changed attitude, as a previous *"spectator"* did: he prayed after returning, *"Lord, I will freely support those missionaries, but please don't ask me to live and work there."*

> <u>8. Finally, you must think the same thoughts, share difficulties with one another, having automatic interdependence with brotherly kindness; be tender-hearted and humble-</u>

minded: 9. you must not repay injury with injury, or hard words with hard words, but bless those who curse you. For you were called to give kind words to others and come to a well-spoken eulogy at the end. 10. **For the one wishing to love life and see prosperous days, let him avoid an evil tongue and cunning words. 11. Habitually avoid evil and do good things; let him seek and follow peace. 12. Because the eyes of the Lord watch over the righteous, and His ears listen to their payers:** but the Lord looks directly into the eyes of wrongdoers. (1 Peter 3:8-12 EDNT)

Austere and Bleak Environment

It is relatively easy to take a "mission trip" with a group of excited believers, but living and working in the same austere and bleak environment overtime is a different story. A visiting 300-pound pastor is remembered riding a burro on a mountain trail in Central America. His feet almost touched the ground and he began to feel for the small burro laboring to carry him and his luggage up the steep trail. He got off the burro but left his suitcase on the animal. After a short walk up the rugged trail, he said to a friend,*" I think I'll just get back on this donkey and help him carry my suitcase."* It was a sight to see: this super-sized preacher straddling a small donkey holding his suitcase to help the little burro with the heavy load. It is doubtful that a picture of this monstrosity would raise any funds for missions. I was thinking, what if God had enabled that donkey to speak to the preacher as happened when *"A dumb donkey spoke with a human voice and ordered the prophet not to speak falsely. (2*

Peter 2:16 EDNT) Had that happened the preacher would have had a whopper of a missionary sermon when he returned to the comfort of his church. *"While on this mission trip, God miraculously spoke to me…etc."*

A Pristine view of Lifestyle

22. You must be honest with yourselves and live by the word not merely hear it. 23. But those who listens to the word, and do not behave it, are similar to a man seeing his own face in a mirror; 24. he observes his flaws, and immediately forgets the man he saw. 25. But whosoever bows down to observe the complete prescriptive usage and the unrestrained opportunity to continue in the word and not become a forgetful hearer, but <u>one who behaves the prescribed deeds, this man shall by the blood be set apart for consecrated action.</u> 26. **If any man among you seems to be devout, and restrains not his unnatural language, he deceives his own heart and his service to God is ineffective.** *(James 1:22-26 EDNT)*

A Pure Missional Lifestyle

James wrote about a pure an unadulterated lifestyle that acted with a missionary perspective. Sanctified eyes that could see each child without the influence of a believing father as being in need of surrogate nurturing. They could observe women alone who lack a husband in their hardship or misfortune that were in need of support and care of an extended family or a man of faith. In addition to doing good for orphans and women alone, those with a missional lifestyle could see spiritual opportunity in each observable circumstance. True evangelism is meeting the needs of hurting individuals and families at the earliest point in time at the farthest distance from the place of worship.

Thinking the way a missionary normally does causes one to see opportunities where others simply see troubles and trials. In the presence of family disfunction and personal difficulties there are opportunities to lead others into the House of God for vertical soul cure and horizontal fellowship. This can truly be "snatching souls" from the hands of Satan and bring them into the Arms of Jesus.

An Unadulterated Missional Leader

27. Free from all that would dim the transparency in belief and conduct before God and the Father is this, **to go see and relieve the orphans without a father's protection and the women lacking a husband in their distress, and to keep himself untainted by the world.** *(James 1:27 EDNT)*

A Second Touch by Jesus

Do we need a special "come to Jesus" moment? All believers need clear vision to see the opportunities placed before them daily. Most churchgoers could use a "second touch" of Jesus to correct their short-sighted vision of both humanitarian and spiritual needs of people. We need to focus on the present needs. The familiar story of a wounded man left by robbers on the roadside, who religious leaders passed by without offering assistance, while a traveling Samaritan both saw and acted on behalf of the urgent personal need of a stranger.

There would most likely be more true celebration at places of worship if more believers behaved as did the Samaritan rather than conducting themselves as others who both witnessed the need and neglected to act at the point of need. Perhaps a second touch by Jesus would produce a moment of true celebration? Mark records a blind man being brought to Jesus.

> *23. And Jesus took the blind man by the hand, and led him outside the village; and dampened his eyes with saliva and laid on His hands, and asked him can you see anything? 24. And the man looked up, and said, <u>I see men as trees, walking.</u>* **25. After that Jesus laid His hands on his eyes again, and his sight came into focus, and he saw every man clearly.** *(Mark 8:23-25 EDNT)*

Scriptural Chronology for Global Evangelism

The Gospels present a chronology of a Divine plan to reach the world with the message of grace. Mark, Luke, and Matthew are known as the Synoptic Gospels meaning *"to see together."* Generally, their material is the same but presented with a different emphasis. **Mark,** considered the oldest Gospel, presents Jesus as an **Active Servant** moving from place to place to complete His work. Forty times Mark wrote that Jesus did this or that and "straightway" or "immediately" moved to another place for additional ministry. Mark is a much better place to start reading the narrative.

Matthew declared to the Jews that Jesus was the Messiah and their King; **Luke** explained to Theophilus *"all that Jesus begin to do and teach"* and that Rome worshiped a man who claimed to be a god and they called him Caesar, but Luke made clear that he and others served a God who became Man, and we call Him Jesus.

John, writing from Ephesus after Christianity was established, obviously felt that the narrative of Jesus needed to be affirmed to the converted Jews and the Gentile world so all would clearly see the Deity of Jesus and accept His authority to bring salvation to the world. John's work was the last of the narratives on the life of Jesus.

Notice the Chronology of the Divine Plan

1. Mark, being the first and oldest gospel, presents Jesus as an example of **Active Servanthood** – As the disciples traveled, they were to follow the example of Jesus and share the good news to the whole of creation. Mark saw God working with human activity as they went forth and preached (witnessed) everywhere.

> 15. And He said, **As you journey to the whole world, proclaim a good message to every inhabitan**t. 16. He who believes and is baptized will be saved; but he who believes not will be condemned. 17. And these miracles will follow those who believe; in My name will they cast out demons; they will speak with unnaturally acquired languages: 18. they may take up serpents; and if they drink **any deadly thing, it will not hurt them; they will lay hands on** the sick, and they will recover. 19<u>. So then after the Lord had spoken to them, He was received up into heaven, and sat on the right hand of God.</u>

*20. **And they with them, and validating the message with***

2. Luke wrote to the Gentile world embodied in the person of "Theophilus" *about all that Jesus begin to do and teach* and that Rome was worshiping a man who claimed to be a god called Caesar. Luke made it clear that I worship a God who became Man and His Name is Jesus. Luke was concerned about human involvement in the divine plan, but emphasized Jesus words, *"Don't go yet, wait to be empowered by the Power of the Spirit.* Luke saw Jesus' followers personally accountable: *"This same Jesus shall return."*

45. Then He opened their understanding, that they might grasp the meaning of the scriptures. 46. And said, Scripture clearly says that Messiah should suffer, and stand up from the grave the third day: 47. and that repentance and forgiveness of sins should be proclaimed in His name among all nations, starting at Jerusalem. **48. And you are witnesses of these things. 49. And, behold, I send the promise of My Father: but you must wait expectantly in Jerusalem, until you be clothed with ability and heavenly st***rength. (Luke 24:45-49 EDNT)*

8. But you shall receive miraculous ability and strength, after the Holy Spirit is come upon you: and you shall be My witnesses unto the death both in Jerusalem, and in all Judaea, and in Samaria, and continually into the farthest part of the earth. *(Acts 1:8 EDNT)*

Luke's second volume, Acts of the Apostles, was a history of the first thirty years of the early church. He was the only Gentile writer in the New Testament. He made an effort to compare Peter and Paul, and so the text of Acts was proportioned equally between these two early leaders. The first half of Acts is all about Peter, the Apostle to the Jews; the last half about Paul, the Apostle to the Gentiles. Luke faithfully compares Peter and Paul in many areas of their life and ministry. However, he always showed the leadership of the Holy Spirit.

3. In **Matthew**'s writing Jesus presents His Challenge to His close Followers. Matthew, who went about the community *collecting taxes, understood the simple instructions of Jesus:* **As you go, do these things**. 1) Make Disciples 2) Identify them with the Godhead through baptism 3) Teach them to behave all the **teachings of Jesus 4) Practice the Presence of Jesus until the** end of the journey.

> *18. And Jesus came and spoke, saying, All authority has been committed to Me in heaven and in earth. 19. *As you personally go (going) therefore, and* **make disciples** *of all* **nations, baptizing them in the name of the Father, and of the Son, and of the Holy Spirit: 20. teaching them to** *observe all things whatever I have commanded you: and behold,* **I am with you always, even unto the end of the world.** *So be it. (Matthew 28:18-20 EDNT)*

4. John was concerned about **the nature and continuity of the mission.** He emphasized Jesus' words *"As the Father sent me, so sent I you."* As one of the original Disciples, John had a much closer relationship with Jesus that the other writers. They basically received their information from others, while John gave a first-hand account as an eye-witness to the earliest activity that convinced many that Jesus was the Messiah. Since the other Gospels were in circulation for over three decades, John took the opportunity to complete his emphasis on the Deity of Jesus. John was concerned that the new converts in the Gentile world had not seen the early miracles of Jesus which supported His authority. He presented the early deeds of Jesus before John the Baptist was imprisoned, while the others gave accounts of the later periods of the ministry of Jesus. To me John was preoccupied with the concept that Jesus personally "sent" others to continue His work and he wanted the present generation to know that their orders came directly for Jesus…"*as you go make disciples."*

2

AMPLIFY Worship Through Celebration

—a vertical experience that recognizes the "worth-ship" of God.

Celebration (Infinity #)

Worship is a Vertical Experience

Worship may mean different things to different people; however, the essence of worship is a realization of the *"worth-ship of God"* and is a vertical experience. Worship has little reference to those present; it is a concentration on the divine through prayer, song, witness, and listening to God from the Word. Any distraction can be a diversion from worship. How much is God worth in your life and your family? How do you value God? Worship is an observance of the redemptive value and personal blessings brought to believers by the death and resurrection of Jesus. True worship is looking at the Cross through the empty tomb and remembering what God has done through His redemptive blessings. Worship is respect for the holy (*respect is to observe and pay attention to*) that which has value in life. Worship can be realized by thoughts of God's grace, singing words of a song, through intercessory prayer, by studying or listening to the Word, and by a moral lifestyle and a clear conscience before God.

Worship may be an individual response to the "worth-ship of God" or a collective expression by 2 or 3 or by hundreds or thousands: there are no limits to the number included in the experience of true worship (two to infinity). *"Where two or three are gathered together, there am I in the midst."* The emphasis is "togetherness" not numbers. Worship becomes a celebration by people of faith. Entertainment, personal excitement or an emotional response are not true expressions of worship. At times God ministers to believers in a *"still small voice."* True worship has lasting results.

Celebration and worship should lead to an individual and collective lifestyle witness and outreach of the Gospel. Believers were saved to serve! When a celebrity walks into a crowded place no one has to prompt a response; it is automatic. How much more when one feels the Presence of God. Why do we think that worshippers have to be prompted and entertained; the "presence" of God should be sufficient to cause believers to show reverence, adulation, and praise to God and celebrate the value or worth-ship of God in their lives. Paul's words:

> *The God you unknowingly worship, I announce to you. 24. The God who ordered the universe and all the things in it, the One being Lord of heaven and earth does not dwell in hand made shrines; 25. neither is He served by human hands, as though He needed something from man, seeing*

He gives to all life, breath, and all things; 26. and has made of one blood all nations of men who dwell on the earth, determined the history of nations and their territory; 27. **so they should search for God and hopefully find Him although He is not far from all of us. 28. For in Him we live and move, and have our being;** (Acts 17:23b-28a EDNT)

"Stand and Await Orders"

Worship is from the heart and prompts behavior that glorifies God. During the Vietnam era Dr. Green was a USAF Reserve Chaplain. Speaking in uniform on a Sunday morning near Dobbins Air Force Base, at the close of the service one could feel the presence of God. A young man in the back quickly stood at attention, braced and stood for a moment then sat. After the benediction, he came quickly to the front and said, "Sir, I am sorry to interrupt your service. I just spent 4 years in the U.S. Marines and when I felt the presence of a superior officer I automatically stood, braced and waited for orders." Would it not be wonderful if the Presence of God were strong enough in a worship service that individuals stood at attention and waited for divine orders.

There would be plenty of volunteers for lifestyle service, sufficient funds to operate the ministry and outreach, and disciplined believers marching together in harmony. Does anyone remember when true Soldiers of the Cross moved as **a mighty army against the strongholds of Satan?**

20. And they went out and witnessed everywhere, the Lord working with them, and validating the message with accompanying supernatural wonders. (Mark 16:20 EDNT)

Celebration embraces the value of God and acknowledges the worth-ship of divine influence in all aspects of life, for the individual and collectively for those gathered. Worshipful celebration is an expression of *agape* love (one-way love that is vertical and spiritually directed toward God and effectively demonstrated daily for the lost). A prayer that survived from the earliest days of Christianity is known as The Apostles Creed:

I Believe in God,

The Father almighty,
Creator of heaven and earth.
I believe in Jesus Christ, His only Son, our Lord,
Who was conceived by the Holy Spirit
And born of the Virgin Mary.
He suffered under Pontius Pilate,
Was crucified, died, and was buried;
He descended into hell.
The third day He rose again from the dead.
He ascended into heaven
And is seated at the right at the right hand of God the Father almighty.
From there He will come to judge the living and the dead.
I believe in the Holy Spirit,
The holy catholic church,
The communion of saints,
The forgiveness of sins,
The resurrection of the body,
And the life everlasting. Amen.

Worship may include confession, collect, communion and celebration. *Confession* is an individual act of admission of human weakness, the acknowledgement of guilt, and the affirmation of forgiveness. *Collect* is the gathering "together" of believers assembled in unity responding to personal pardon and the promises of God; this is personal prayer, praise and worship. *Communion* is born again believers walking in fellowship with God and others commemorating the death and resurrection of Jesus; it included what the Greeks called *"koinonia" and* transliterated as *communion, community, joint participation, stewardship, sharing, and spiritual intimacy.*

The first use of *koinonia* was in Peter's sermon at Pentecost (Acts 2:41-47) where the essence of *koinonia* was love, faith, and encouragement. Also, Paul used the concept to express agreement with one another, being united in purpose, and serving alongside each other based on fellowship with God and each other. (Philippians 2:1-11). Communion clearly expresses shared beliefs and common expectations. It also suggests closeness of relationship and remembrance of the death, burial and resurrection of Jesus.

> .... *Rescue yourselves from this troublesome generation. 41.* **Those who willingly received His Word, were baptized**: <u>and the same day about three thousand souls were added to the believers. 42. And</u> **they continued consistently in the apostles' doctrine and fellowship, and in breaking of bread, and in prayers**. *43. Everyone was filled with a sense of reverence: and many signs and wonders were done by the apostles. 44. All who believed kept together, and*

all their possessions were shared; 45. Goods and property were sold and distributed as every man had need. **46. And they agreed to meet daily in the temple and to break bread from house to house, and they took meals cheerfully and with personal commitment. 47. Praising God and having favor with all the people. And the Lord added to the church daily those being saved.** *(Acts 2:40-47 EDNT)*

1. If there be any **encouragement** *in Christ, if any* **reassurance in love**, *if any* **participation of the Spirit**, *if any* **tenderness and compassion**, *2. fill up my joy by* **living in harmony, having the same love, being in one accord of one mind.** *3. Let nothing be done through argument or excessive pride; but in true humility let each value others more than themselves. 4.* **Look not after your own interests, but practice looking after the interest of others. 5. Let your disposition and thoughts be the same as Christ Jesus:** *6. although having a divine nature, did not cling to His equality with God: 7. but stripped Himself of His rightful divinity, and took upon Himself the nature of a servant, and was made in the likeness of men: 8. and appearing in human form, He humbled Himself, and became obedient even to death on the cross. 9.* **Wherefore God highly exalted Him, and gave Him a name that is above every name: 10. that at the name of Jesus every knee**

should bow, in heaven, and in earth, and things under the earth; 11. and that every tongue should openly confess that Jesus Christ is Lord, to the glory of God the Father.
(Philippians 2:1-11 EDNT)

Fellowship among Believers

Congregation is a subset of Celebration with between (40-120) participants gathered for fellowship, identified by family, interest, friendship, and closeness. In a small or established place of worship, Celebration and Congregation may be interchangeable; however, leadership must arrange for both functions: worship and fellowship. Congregation is a subset unit of Celebration that is a cohesive expression of *philia.* Philadelphia-type "brotherly love" which creates a feeling of togetherness. This closeness was called "*homothumadon*" by the Greeks, meaning *one mind, one accord, one passion, in one place.*

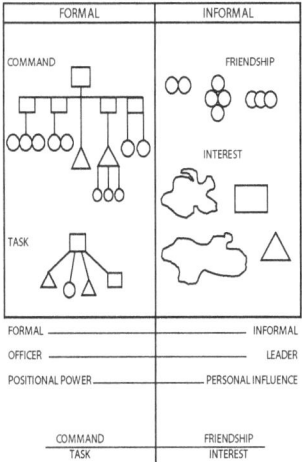

Congregations <u>40 – 120</u> people

Mixing Groups becomes Problematic

As new and small groups (congregations) form within the existing constituency, they become observable and distinct and often exclusive. As the congregants increase in numbers, mixing Celebration and Congregation meetings becomes more problematic. As multiple congregations develop based on friendship, kinship, and interest groups in the same arena, the programming becomes almost self-defeating. This is one reason many churches never consistently reach more that 40 to 120 people on Sunday morning. In extremely large gatherings, there is a straight forward effort to direct the attention by the leadership vertically away from other people attending the meeting. *"The more the merrier"* adage does not assure a vertical service of worship that points the congregants to the "worth-ship" of God in their lives while they are dealing with personal interaction with those around them. Times of fellowship and closeness need to be programmed separately. This requires an understand of the biblical perspective on gatherings, a grasp of group dynamics and a clear knowledge of organizational sociology, as well as the guidance of the Holy Spirit.

> *41. Those who willingly received his word, were baptized: and the same day about three thousand souls were added to the believers. 42. And they continued consistently in the apostles' doctrine and fellowship, and in breaking of bread, and in prayers. 43. Everyone was filled with a sense of reverence: and many signs and wonders were done by the apostles. 44. All who believed kept together, and all their possessions*

were shared; 45. Goods and property were sold and distributed as every man had need. 46. **And they agreed to meet daily in the temple and to break bread from house to house, and they took meals cheerfully and with personal commitment. 47. Praising God and having favor with all the people. And the Lord added to the church daily those being saved.** *(Acts 2:41-47 EDNT)*

Perhaps we should remember that Jesus was from Galilee and the original Twelve Apostles were all from Galilee. Even the replacement of Judas was from Galilee. Also, the 120 in the Upper Room were all considered to be Galileans although a few were from other locations. The others had been fully acculturated and were seen as Galileans. This is called homogenous grouping and the words used to describe such a group are: *similar, equal, identical, harmonized, all the same.*

It appears that the daily gatherings at the Temple or local synagogues outside of Jerusalem were different than the Sabbath service. There were always prayers and reading of the Torah and discussions that followed, because the people did not have personal copies of the Torah. Early converts, being Jewish, availed themselves of the tradition of frequent visits to the temple or the local synagogues; they were the only communal places available. Since the early leaders were brought up in Jewish traditions, they naturally went to where Jewish people gathered; it was part of their "Jews first" strategy.

17:1 And traveling through Amphipolis and Apollonia, they came to Thessalonica, where the Jews had a synagogue: 2. and Paul following his custom, went to the synagogue and for three Sabbaths reasoned with them out of the scriptures, 3. openly affirming, that it was necessary for Christ to suffer death and stand up again from the grave; and that this Jesus, whom I declare to you, is the Christ. (Acts 17:1-4 EDNT)

Unlike the later synagogues after the destruction of the Temple in AD 70, local synagogues were public meeting places with benches along the walls: a kind of Jewish community center and a lodging place for travelers. In addition to reading the Torah and prayers, there was teaching and discussion about what was read. It is worthy of note that the early apostles understood the necessity for personal worship in the Temple, where there were multiple groups with various connections and allergenics, from their house to house teaching and preaching where there were family and friends. Clearly, they were adjusting and directing their teaching and preaching to the needs of the audience at different gatherings.

Regardless of the size, or when and where believers gather, there are needs that must be met and the program and the message should be tailored to the needs of those present. This certainly speaks to the lack of relevance of most sermons in the worship service when it is directed to a few "sinners" or "a few weak saints" instead of ministering to the needs of the larger group. The normal explanation: this is the only opportunity to speak to some issues because the church has combined the schedule for the convenience of leaders and at the expense of the individual needs.

However, when the needs of a few are dealt with in a public service it is evident that the pastoral watch care of souls and believers outreach evangelism is not adequately working.

Spiritual leadership must get back to personal and private interaction with those in need of guidance and minister to the general needs for growth and development of the constituency in regular services. Public and collective counseling of a few at the expense of many is certainly not the best use of the people's time or pastoral responsibility. It appears that this becomes necessary because *"this is the only time they are here!"* When in reality most of such issues could be handled by individuals at other places and at other times. When unsaved individuals and believers with personal problems make it to the sanctuary still in need, it becomes evident that the local cure and care of souls is being neglected by the band of believers. Provided these issues were cared for otherwise, the Celebration could be a true observance of worship directed toward God and His worth and the value-added to the individuals and body of believers.

Some years ago, Dr. Green wrote a book, Why Wait till Sunday? This was after interviewing pastors about their philosophy of ministry. Some clearly stated, *"I try to do it all on Sunday morning, because that is the only time the people are here."* Then the big question was asked, *What about the rest of the week?* The answer, *"I just set on the porch and wait on Sunday."* Most gave no attention to the pattern established in the New Testament.

> *42. And every day* **in the temple and in every house, they ceased not to teach and preach** *Jesus Christ. (Acts 5:42 EDNT)*

Multiple Congregations

There will be more than one congregation included in the Celebration at larger gatherings. This is depending on the size and make-up of the constituency. Data about the study of the social consciousness and emotional structures and direct experience relative to this self-motivated phenomena in faith-based worship, spiritual gatherings, family renewal, and the whole field of religion, ethics, and morality will be noted in the following chapters. Meanwhile, let us more clearly understand the difference in Celebration and Congregation.

Provided church leaders clearly understand the difference between worship and fellowship, most existing places of worship could be expanded through sincere efforts to engage the church family and the community by gathering kinship groups and friends with common values and interest into events where there is shared fellowship and a genuine connection with friends. Such congregational-type meetings will enhance the possibility of new friends and acquaintances becoming part of the Congregation. The congregation must again become a gathering of family and friends for fellowship and togetherness to experience the dynamics of spiritual togetherness in full agreement in one place.

An Interactive Fellowship

A service of Celebration differs drastically at the personal level with the nature of interactions among members of a group of family and friends which is how one defines a Congregation. The difference is clear, Congregation is an interactive fellowship activity of gathered and compatible individuals who share common space and time with family and friends. It is where individuals pay attention to those around them and enjoy a combined experience with friends through spiritual fellowship.

On the other hand, Celebration may appear to be a private gathering of strangers where individuals evaluate those present and become protective of both their personal and social space. Celebration is a time to concentrate on the value of God in life and living; not fellowship with strangers. This is why Celebration is an individual and vertical experience where attention is given to the words of songs, the reading and preaching of the Word and celebrating the presence of God in the lives of the people.

> *23.The God you unknowingly worship, I announce to you. 24. The God who ordered the universe and all the things in it, the One being Lord of heaven and earth* **does not dwell in hand made shrines; 25. neither is He served by human hands, as though He needed something from man**, *seeing He gives to all life, breath, and all things; 26. and has made of one blood all nations of men who dwell on the earth, determined the history of nations and their territory; 27*. **so they should search for God and hopefully find Him although He is not far from all of us. 28. For in Him we live and move and have our being;** *as certain also of your own poets have said, For we are also His offspring. 29.* **Since we are the offspring of God, we ought not to think that the Deity has any similarity to anything made of gold,**

silver, or stone that is sculptured by the art and imagination of man. *(Acts 17:23-29 EDNT)*

A Personalized Approach to Worship

At Celebration churchgoers internalize their needs and personalize their individual approach to the worship of God and resist an intrusion from others especially strangers. The personal interactive intricacies and restraints at work in spiritual worship become a freeze-frame view similar to one person watching a televised worship service in the privacy of their home. When like-minded individuals gather together in combination of personal joy and group fellowship, they remain individuals. Congregation is a gathering of like-minded souls who enjoy association with others through a kinship-type of response normally known as camaraderie, which is mutual trust and friendship among people who spend a lot of time together. It is a feeling of pride, fellowship and/or shared loyalty among friends. This is interaction at the human level and is one step below the personal worship of God. True worship requires individual attention to the words of songs and the Word of God without the distraction or intrusion on their mind or personal space by intruding strangers.

Rules of "Personal Space"

The space immediately surrounding someone is known as "personal space" and encroachment on this area causes one to feel threatened or uncomfortable. This space is defined as "intimate" about 18 inches and "personal" from 1½ to 4 feet where only friends and acquaintances are welcome. Strangers are strictly forbidden in the intimate and personal space. Then, there is "social space" which extends from 4 to 12 feet where people feel comfortable interacting with acquaintances and friends. It is easy to see that the rules of "personal space" are at work in Celebration and Congregation as individual believers and groups respond in the presence of others to the presence of God. Most women prefer not to be hugged by strange men in church. Some men cannot handle a beautiful young lady within their intimate space. A personal experience in the early ministry of Dr. Green is a reminder of the care young preachers must take in all relationships.

After ministering in a Jacksonville Church, standing with the pastor, H. G. Poitier, at the rear of the black church while several beautiful young ladies in the line began to hug the old pastor. He was a handsome old gentleman, Sidney Poitier's uncle, and had been their pastor for many years. They had grown up under his ministry, so they gave him a full bosom grandfather hug. As they came to me, I took a step back and extended my hand. Some reluctantly shook my hand, but one beautiful black lady insisted on hugging me. I said, *"I'm not sure my ordination can handle such a hug!"* Her response was clear: "*You white folks make sin out of everything!*" Agreeing that ministers sometimes erred on the side of caution. She mumbled something sounding like, "*You white folks can't tell the difference between Christian love and that other stuff.*" All the old preachers who spoke to me during my early ministry always cautioned about over familiarity with females. My thoughts were **"...it's better to be safe than sorry."**

History Speaks Frankly on Decline

A report in The *Washington Post (2013)* stated that more people prayed than believed in God. History of the American church speaks frankly about the decline of morality and the loss of churchgoers. It considered causes and consequences of the problem, but offered no solutions. In times past, many churches were a small gathering of family and friends and services of worship were preceded by Sunday school classes which served the fellowship needs of the people before they entered the morning service. Earlier congregational fellowship enhanced the atmosphere of Celebration in worship by meeting the social and fellowship needs before the people arrived for Celebration. There were several distinct services and activities on the Calendar that served different needs of the family and individuals from the community.

Sunday school classes preceded the worship service and created a social and interactive environment. The Sunday morning service was a celebration of personal salvation, the blessings of God on the family, the excitement of singing, and where people were enriched by preaching that pointed them to God and away from their surroundings and personal issues. Celebration directed individuals vertically to the words of hymns, the reading of Old and New Testament passages and the anointed ministry that acknowledged God's blessings.

Sunday evening was given to testimony, fellowship and mid-week provided meetings for prayer and Bible study. There were occasional classes for new converts and young converts growing into disciples, but no serious effort to educate the new constituency in biblical content or the principles of a missional lifestyle. Some scheduled special revival services and activities for the youth and planned events for children without the benefits of a learning center for community and family education. There was a busyness of activities, but the church did not grow because many of the dynamics of personal and group needs for interactions were not fully understood by those in charge. Actually, some well-meaning activities hindered the growth of the constituency.

Churchgoers became Spectators

The impact of two World Wars, the increase of both parents working, latch-key children, notes on the refrigerator, children growing up and becoming involved in higher education, the culture of society and the complexity of family life intruded on participation in worship. Gradually churchgoers became spectators and attendance declined. It takes a lot of effort to entertain and/or excite spectators. Consequently, churches began to a combine scheduled services on Sunday and the mixture of celebration and congregation attempted to accommodate attendance decline. The combined schedule began sending adults one direction and children another; spouses were separated into specialized classes and children were graded by age: the family was divided and family worship and the sense of "gathering together" was diminished. Churches moved from being a gathering of family and friends to gradually becoming a gathering of other people. Yet those in charge did not change their mindset to accommodate the new and developing needs. Individual needs and family issues were not being adequately met. Many leaders did not understand the dynamics at work in the personal and group interactions and individuals often felt left out or unfilled. This exacerbated the attendance decline.

This sparked further negative participation and attendance continued to decline. Church attendance is a volunteer activity and unless one clearly receives "something personal" that enhances their life or meets some personal goal, they may choose not to return. The negative suspicions and gossip provide faulty reasons for this failure and create further difficulties for leadership.

The teaching ministry was weakened and gradually was being replaced by entertainment and weak showmanship to attract attendance, true worship and real fellowship continued to suffer. Congregants began a rapid search for a place or activity that met their personal and spiritual needs. Some turned to smaller or larger churches, others to radio and television; still others visited "house-type" prayer and bible studies, while others simply disassociated themselves from all organized religion. Many who still claimed an association with God did not feel the need to participate in public worship or continue involvement with a local fellowship or any community faith-based group.

Decline Prompted new Programming

This decline prompted a search for new programming to attract attendance. Gradually, the church scene became classified as small, average, large and mega. Attendance for a small church was under 50, while the average attendance for the next group was from 40 to 120 on Sunday morning; then it jumped to larger gatherings where attendance averaged from 500 to 2,000; finally, a few mega churches sprang up and began gathering up large numbers of dropouts, dissatisfied strays and spectators from the declining churches. Of course, this does not count the number who stay home and passively listened to a radio broadcast or watched the "show" at some Televangelist Chapel or were entertained by a Hollywood theater production at the Holy Television Cathedral on a cable network. This prompted small churches to experiment with new programming in an effort to coach dropouts back to the fold. Well, there goes the neighborhood and places of worship along with the family table, bible study, altar, car, and the family pew. Individuals and families began to twist in the wind of a secular society.

However, smart phones, texting and electronic gimmicks together with Facebook, emails, Tweets, and computer apps replaced the gathering of family and friends to meet the social needs for a sense of connectedness. Notes on the refrigerator and electronic texting of messages replaced family conversation and individuals again were alone in a complex world without purpose or spiritual guidance from family or anointed spiritual leadership.

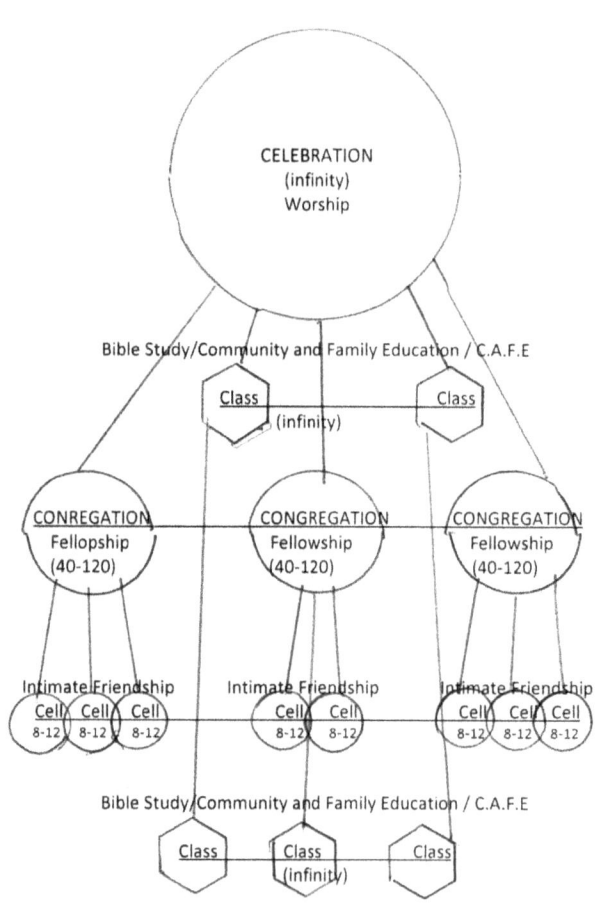

||||||||||||||||||||||||||||||||||||||||||||||||||||
CELEBRATION (infinity) Worship
CONGREGATION (40-120) Fellowship
Cell (8-12) Intimate Friendship [evangelism/spiritual growth]
Class (infinity) Bible Study/Community and Family Education / C.A.F.E.

3

EXPAND Fellowship By Congregational Activity

— a gathering of kinship groups and friends with common interest and values for fellowship.

A Close Fellowship

Congregations begin as a close fellowship unit and as the number increases it becomes more complex based on the interaction among individuals and the selfishness of human relations that commonly exist in groups. Individuals become part of a group when they believe their personal goals will be met when the group attains their objectives. When this does not happen quickly, the complaining begins, and negative participation is the ultimate result. This is why individuals drop out of group activity…they do not see their personal wishes and goals being met by the gathering; therefore, they seek another venue for fulfillment.

Friend are a Valued Asset

Friendship is a valued relationship, in fact, friends are better than money in the bank because one may receive interest from the friendship source without decreasing the total value of the relationship. Another view of friendship problems was explained by a friend *"We are not quite friends. We keep trying, but life get in the way."* An old preacher defined "fellowship" *as "two fellows in the same ship, but not a battleship."* The Old Testament records a question of wounds, the answer *"These are wounds I received in the house of my friends."* (Zechariah 13:6) Friends, even family, can break your heart and cause more hurt than an enemy. As one man explained, *"If you have friends like that you sure don't need any enemies!"* Even the silence of a friend may hurt worse than deliberate action by an adversary or competitor.

Human Interaction can be Difficult

All interaction between people can be difficult, and are divided into personal, interpersonal and intrapersonal communication issues. In the sender, receiver, and feedback model there is static that comes from the root or core of a response which interferes with understanding the message. Intrapersonal response comes from mind and culture of the sender, while interpersonal communication is filled with verbal and nonverbal cues used to accomplish the sender's goals. Then there are the personal expectations and issues of the receiver in reading the person or decoding the message. This is why both verbal and nonverbal messages are being communicated between all persons in a faith-based congregation. The tone of voice, the facial expressions, body language, dress, habitual mannerism, and ways of behaving all send clues as to whether a person is open and willing to accept others into their circle of friends. In similar fashion, individuals send a message of their willingness to become a participant in the activities of the meeting or gathering.

Sophisticated and Complicated

Human relationships are both sophisticated and complicated. Past experiences, knowledge, traditions and culture create a sophistication that can only be penetrated by following certain rules of interpersonal relationships. Having a grasp of the complicated nature of human interaction and personal communication can improve the positive behavior in any situation. Personal relationships are further complicated by present circumstances, unforeseen difficulties, man-made obstacles, and extended family and/or personnel issues. And of course, at times, the actions and words of friends.

Connected and Interacting

Becoming relational is an attitude about the way two or more individuals are connected and presently interact. This attitude creates a predisposition to behave in a certain way toward others and becomes relational behavior that is easily observed. The difficulty of developing close and personal relationships is the complication of the addition of a third party to a relationship or the nature of group interaction that impacts individual behavior. There is a formula to explain this complication; it is simple, scientific and determines how the increase of numbers of interactions in a relationship can bring complications. The interactive relationship formula is [**R= n x (n-1)**] ; in words *[number - times -(number minus 1) equals number of interactions and/or interpersonal relationships].*

Complexity of Relationships are Relative to Size

A couple is just two people and except for the baggage they bring to the relationship, it is simple when compared with larger groups. Add four parents to the couple and you have 6 x (6-1) = 30 interpersonal interactions happening. When each have siblings, the relationship is further complicated. Adding a third party to a couple's relationship adds more complication *"two is a couple, but three is a crowd."* One can readily see how adding others complicates personal relationships. Think of planning a wedding: the couple is being advised by two extended families plus as many as 100 close friends. This would include parents, grandparents, siblings, and friends and increases the number to about 125 people. [125 x (125--1) = 15,500] interpersonal interactions.

No wonder some couples just secretly elope to avoid the confusion of multiple points of view. This could also explain the hurt feelings which come from such interactions. This may also explain the continuing problem of "in laws" in some marriages. These facts are clearly illustrated by the frustration seen on the face of a bride-to-be at rehearsal with so many intruding on her personal space constantly sharing *"how things are supposed to be done."* When will we learn and follow Paul's advice, *"Study to be quiet and mind your own business."*

Nonverbal Cues are Important

The nonverbal cues must be observed in all gatherings by those in charge. Forces that stimulate growth and change are present in all faith-based congregations as the dynamics of social change works;

this is just human nature. Leadership must have a clear understanding of these forces to recognize and channel changes toward positive transformation and spiritual growth of the constituency. Since a Congregation is made up of (40 –120) people, consider the complications in personal interactions and relationships. Apply the formula to the small number of forty [40 x (40 – 1) = 1,560 interactions]; now apply to the larger number of one-hundred and twenty [120 x (120 – 1) = 14,280 interactions]. Growth has its problems, and these must be solved to sustain development.

The observable difficulties increase as the congregation grows. This accounts for the large number of independent sectarian groups, denominations, local congregations, and the many small faith-based worship centers. One Lord, One Faith and One Baptism has become a stewpot of personal opinions and individual perspectives which requires a clear understanding of organizational dynamics by prepared and spiritual leadership. Spiritual maturity among those gathered is a plus the value of which cannot be measured.

Understanding the Changes in a Convert's Life

Adjustment is slow and at times painful in new relationships. Moving though the stages may take five minutes, five hours, five days, or five months, no one can predict. Whether it is a new personal relationship or a new convert or a new church member, all will go through these stages (1) Form, (2) Storm, (3) Norm, and (4) Perform in adjusting their attitude and behavior to a new environment or building new associations and connections with other believers for fellowship and support. It is a relational process and it is constantly working.

CYCLE OF RELATIONSHIP

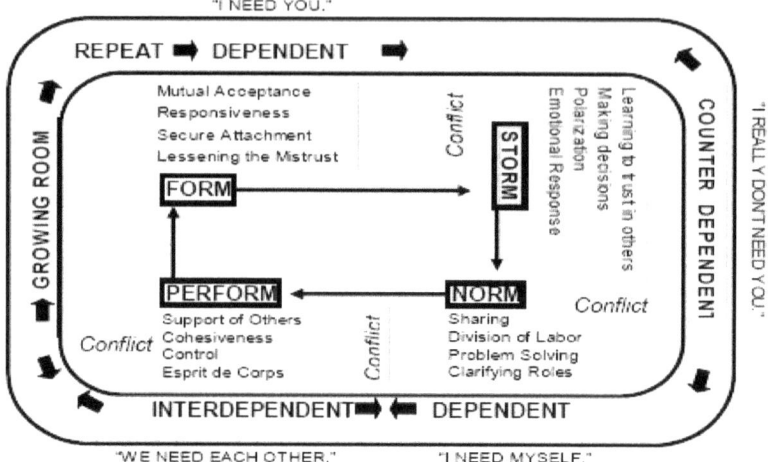

- *Conflict occurs between each phase. No gain without pain.*
- *Conflict resolution is required to proceed to the next phase.*

Working with New Converts and New Members

The behavior of a disciple maker, spiritual mentor or life coach following a convert's initial encounter with Christ or a new member added to the congregation will change as the individual proceeds through these stages. The first stage behavior of the mentor or coach should be (1) **Telling** (High Task/low relationship). Normally, one would think the obvious would be High Relationship/low task, but providing things to "do" simple activities, such as a short prayer, completing a data form (name, age, address, family information, etc.) will show the spiritual leader's interest and that the person is important.

An early task to introduce new people to other believers of their age is a good way to transition into new surroundings. This attention must be age-specific, different attention for different people. Until the spiritual leader knows and understands the person better, it is best to be busy "doing things" instead of just face-to-face talking. When a new person is in stage one emotionally, they are (dependent); the mentor or coach must "tell" them the things they need to know so they can begin to feel the first stage motion of (1) **"I need you."**

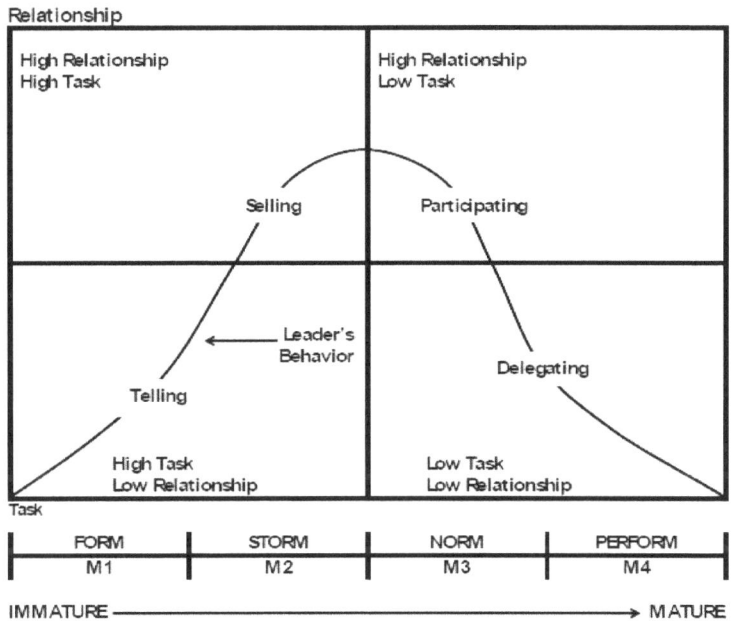

The range of emotions in the new convert or new members will be: (1) **"I Need You!"** (2) **"I Really Don't Need You."** (3) **"I Need Myself."** (4) **"We Need Each Other."** If one identified the stages above as 1, 2, 3, and 4, the response attitude of the convert is (1) **Form Stage** -- Dependent, "I need you!" (2) **Storm Stage** -- Counter-dependent, "I really don't need you." (3) **Norm Stage** -- Independent, "I need myself." and (4) **Perform Stage** -- Interdependent "We need each other!" Naturally, stage four is the goal, but the emotional roller coaster ride and relationship cycle must pass through the other stages as well.

Knowing exactly the stage of the new person is in at a given time is required for the spiritual leader to carefully choose their own behavior: (1) **Telling** (High task/low relationship), (2) Selling (High Task/High Relationship), (3) **Participating** (High relationship/low task), or (4) **Delegating** (low relationship/low task).

All Growth Follows an S-curve

All growth, a human infant, an elephant, a tree, or even social entities such as the stock market, grow and develop in a clear S-curve. An understanding of the S-curve of growth that the life of all organisms, groups and organizations demonstrate is essential to those who would adequately care for new entries into a cell or group. The S-curve of growth has three phases: a period called **the lag phase** (I) when preparation and a framework is being made for growth. The period of actual growth is called **exponential or logarithmic phase** (II). This period of rapid growth and development climaxed in maximum efficiency and usually gives way to a healthy development through a constructive coordination of differing facets of the individual into a uniform whole. At this point in development **a stationary phase** (III) usually develops because of the effort of the individual to survive and maintain basic identity. When the crisis is not met, the energies and resources normally used for growth and development are re-channeled to maintain *status quo*; thus, the leveling off period is entered, when growth ceases and development stabilizes. This is usually called the **stationary phase** and is the most critical. Unless this phase is handled properly, decline begins.

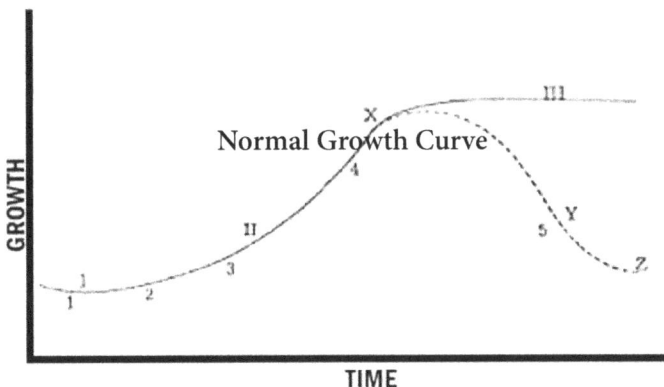

Diagram of the normal growth curve above is for all growth: I-lag phase, II-logarithmic phase, III-stationary phase, X-point of crisis. The Y represents decreased development and the Z points to fixed development below potential. The third stage is a period of stationary where development appears to stop or level off. This is the point of crisis and mentors and coaches must maintain high relationship and high task to move new people forward. After a person reaches point X depending on time or age, the Y and Z may be beyond the domain of the mentor or coach. This is why all available time early on must be given to quality care and planting the seeds of achievement for the future. Ancient sacred writings made it clear that when the young were "trained" properly they would maintain an awareness of early instructions even as they developed more fully.

All growing entities have **a lag phase** early in life when it seems they are not growing. Then **a logarithmic phase** of rapid growth begins that may appear to be exponential. Numbers 1-5 are the normal stages of human development: (1) a weak entry into the real world from the womb, (2) a formal structure and routine for life is established, (3) a period of mental, physical, spiritual and social growth happens, (4) a more formal developmental stage becomes obvious, and (5) if one is not careful there will be a disintegration of concepts and constructs that brought about growth and development as the individual reverts to previous habits and routine. This is the real and continuing difficulty in custodial care of children or the watch care of souls in a spiritual environment and weakness at this point causes most of the failures. Do not be disturbed by this normal process. Keep the following prayer always in your mind.

> Lord, help me to remember that nothing will happen to me today that you and I together can't handle!

The Spiritual Leader's behavior follows the bell curve. The spiritual leader's behavior is traced by the bell curve, it moves from Telling, to Selling, to Participating, and finally to Delegating. These are responses to the levels of maturity at a given time and place. A closer review of the stages will improve an understanding of the process.

People are smart, if caregivers pay too much personal attention to a newcomer, you may send the wrong message. Remember, some people have difficulty with "close personal encounters." At times this attention must be age-specific; through the other stages

Stages of Relationship Building

Understanding the stages of relationship will assist the Mentor or coach in friendship building with a positive outcome. Relational and individual dynamics are prerequisite to effective relationship building with mew people. Although the Cycle of Relationship chart primarily is about a more formal relationship building process, developing a growing friendship with new converts or members is similar and one can learn from the chart. The process does not always go forward. Certain events or changes can cause a person in the Norm or Perform stage to reset to Storm stage. It is difficult to know all the things that create this plunge backward, but it happens. When it does, the caregiver must go back to Form stage behavior (**Telling -- High Task/low relationship**) and move through the process again slowly.

Form Stage is the dependent phase of the relationship. There must be a mutual acceptance on the part of both the caregiver and the new person for the Form Stage to begin. The objective is a mutual responsiveness. At this point the caregiver must establish rapport and find a point of secure attachment. This normally requires a conversation topic or activity that is of interest to the person. During this stage the caregiver is "telling" the new person all the things that will lessen their mistrust of the new experience and environment. The caregiver must be seen as an affectionate benefactor to create the "I need you" response which demonstrates that the person has accepted the first step in integration into the new situation. Hopefully, this "I need you" stage will last a while, but one never knows. It may last five minutes or five hours, then all the garbage breaks loose, and the individual goes into Storm Stage.

Storm Stage is a counter-dependent phase. The person is not sure the new environment and relationships will be beneficial. The dependent attitude was expressed as "I need you!" now the individual feels "**I really don't need you**" and expresses this attitude through some emotional response. This is an emotional response and the mentor or coach must be both kind and gentle, but always High Relationship and High Task. Usually a lack of positive response is out of a lack of knowledge and interpersonal conflict; the caregiver must respond with affection and concern.

The mentor or coach must recognize the Storm Stage and respond to the needs of the individual. Storm stage behavior requires the caregiver to add to the "telling" a kind of **"selling"** with the sharing of some good news and deciding on something to "do" quickly that can get the person's attention away from the feeling of rage or abstract disappointment. The individual has moved to the counter dependent stage and the caregiver must "sell" the positive benefits of the new relationship by saying and doing things the person understands. If the person accepts the approach, makes a decision to permit the interaction, and the emotional response is properly answered, the interaction becomes more normal. However, the individual is vulnerable and remains unstable, so the caregiver must remain attentive and continue a conversation.

At this point it may be best to permit the person to regress to Form Stage with the response attitude of "I need you!" rather than moving on to the Norm sage. At least this buys some time and provides a season of peace and rest. It may take days or months to reach the **Norm Stage**, so do not rush the process. Norm Stage is a participating phase, a time when both the mentor or coach and the individual can journey together in an agreed upon direction doing things that mutually benefit the relationship. This is where the person begins to mature and spiritually grow, thinking for themselves and initiating activities in which they feel totally comfortable.

Actually, an independent relationship develops when the individual's attitude is "I need myself." This is progress. A caregiver must not see it as a negative phase or rebellion; it is a natural part of developing.

During the **Norm Stage** which is a period of walking together, the caregiver "participates" in the life and activities of the person as best they can and walks along and shares the journey without intrusion or direction. This mode is **a ministry of presence and participation; it** is a good place to be in in the process. This, of course, is done in many different ways. An appropriate way forward must be selected from several options. To maintain the norm stage, the individual's larger group relationship and the spiritual development of church life must be considered and dealt with in a positive way. Individuals do not give up longstanding friends for a new connection that is not yet proven to be beneficial. This stage requires problem solving, clarifying of roles, and positive sharing to move to a respondent attitude of "**We need each other.**" Overall, little can be done about the individual's real spiritual development and growth until they come to possess the "**We need each other**" disposition. This is the Perform Stage.

Perform Stage is an interdependent phase where the obvious attitude is "We need each other." When this occurs, the relationship is cemented and can grow as both parties are supported. An *esprit de corps* develops with new friendships. This is a kind of "can do" spirit, a sense of pride expressed in common interest and activities. When this occurs, the relationship has moved into the interdependent phase and needs additional effort to maintain. Normally at this point, the new person is delegated to handle more decisions about their learning activities, and more active in spiritual participation in services. This is a constructive phase, but most likely will not last. Something will happen, or someone will unknowingly do something that triggers a retreat to the Storm Stage behavior of **"I really don't need you"** and an attitude of counter dependence will happen. This is why growing disciples is not an easy process.

No "Group Think"

Forceful elements of interpersonal relationships are at work in each congregation. Scripture is clear that the Word of God came not by the will of man, but directly from the Holy Spirit; consequently, there are no private or personal *"rhema"* interpretation of scripture. The Bible means exactly and only what the first people who heard it understood it to mean; not what the carnal mind or the theologically trained minister says that others think it means. There is no "group think" when it comes to scripture; this is why a congregation of faith must be led by persons who are submissive to the Spirit, have knowledge of the Word, and maintain a humble and teachable spirit. The authority is in the Word not the mind or culture of the reader or interpreter. Even Jesus stood up to read from the Word in Isaiah, because the authority is in the Word not the person reading. This is why the original language of *koine* Greek is important to the study of the Word. The question is what did the

Greek word mean *then* and how can it best be expressed *now* in common language.

Greeks had Four Words — English has One

Ancient Greeks used four distinct words to express affection, attraction, or love. *Agape* was one-way love; *philia* was two-way love; *storge* was used for family love; *eros* was an expression of romantic or physical attraction. *Eros* was not used in the New Testament and has been associated by some only with sexual feelings. Actually, it also expresses an appreciation for the beauty within a person. One must go back to Genesis for "male/female" interaction that fulfills God's instruction to Adam and Eve *"be fruitful and replenish the earth."* The New Testament informs relationships and our personal attraction to perceived beauty becomes attachment normally called intimacy or marriage in a civil society. The process of establishing wedlock differs in various cultures globally.

The Relationship Factor of Scripture

Sacred scripture is a book of personal interactions and moral relationships; not a codified set of doctrines to control every aspect of life and living. There are many teachings that have been gathered and collected as tenants of the faith and others have been grouped or gathered together to form sectarian doctrine. This specificity and hardening of the scriptural teachings has caused a loving God to appear severe and less sympathetic to the commonalities and harmonies of the human race. Consequently, many miss the relationship factor of scriptural intent. This is a great hinderance to faith-based worship and congregational fellowship.

The New Testament was originally presented in *koine* or common Greek that was spoken by the poor and used in ordinary or familiar conversation; it was not academic or literary. In the Original *koine* Greek, the scripture was relational and not presented in harsh or "must" statements. In fact, sin was presented in terms of relationship: if you hate your brother you were guilty of murder; if you bear false witness against your neighbor you were in danger of hell fire; if you covet another's possessions you were guilty of idolatry; sexual activity in one context was sinful while the same act with the same person in a long-term commitment was sanctified. This is why parents should teach their children the reason for their sexual identity: to become a spouse and a parent. Therefore, one looks at a brother or sister differently than a stranger who may become a future soul mate.

God is One but Three
Co-eternal, Co-existing Persons

Why would scripture present the One God as three distinct personalities if believers were not expected to relate differently to each member of the Triune God? Christianity holds that God is one but three co-eternal, co-existing Persons – the Father, the Son, and the Holy Spirit. Christian baptism for converts was designed to identify new believers with the authority of the Father, Son, and the Holy Spirit. This has been neglected along with the sectarian codification of basic teachings of scripture and believers fail to grasp the value of a relationship with the Trinity. To see the Father as a loving forgiver, to know the Son as a Savior and Friend, and to experience the work of the Spirit as a guide, enabler, protector, and a present-day Power for kingdom advance is to short-change those who seek to fully know God.

A String of Pearls

The whole Bible is a string of pearls held together by a blood line. From the creation of the universe, God, the Father designed a plan to bring human beings into close fellowship with Him and to enjoy His blessings forever. Knowing all things, the Son was to be as a Lamb slain from the foundation of the world for the remission of sins, and the Spirit who moved on the waters at creation was to convict the world of sin, righteousness and judgment. After the Fall in the Garden, the Father became the God of another chance to be known as the Forgiver based on a system of blood sacrifices. From Creation to the birth of Jesus, the Godhead communicated with the human race through the Father. At the birth of Jesus (the Messiah) to His Ascension back to heaven, the Living Word was the message to man. With the Ascension Jesus took His seat at the Right Hand of the Father as the only "go between" God and man. This role for Jesus was determined prior to Creation and His role and the New Testament guide for believers were sealed with His shed blood at Calvary. From the Ascension of Jesus until the present time, the Holy Spirit has directed and empowered believers to maintain a missional lifestyle witness to the farthest parts of the earth.

This is the construct for *martyr* or **those who give their lives for a cause.** Those who die for the cause are called a "*martyr*," in reality, they died because they were a *martyr* (a lifestyle witness until the death). Jesus shared with His followers,*"as you go into all the world, make disciples" but wait in Jerusalem and "you shall receive* *miraculous ability and strength, after the Holy Spirit (is) come upon you;* **and you shall be My witnesses unto the death…***"* (Matthew 28:19,20; Acts 1:8 EDNT)

Where are the lifestyle witnesses committed to carry the Gospel to the farthest places? Where is such commitment that causes believers to hazard their life for the gospel? Where are the Heroes of Faith? Some special cure and care of souls are required to develop true witnesses.

> *25. it seemed good, being assembled with one accord, to send chosen men to you with our beloved Barnabas and Paul; 26. men* **who have risked their lives for the name of the Lord Jesus Christ.** *(Acts 15:25-26 EDNT)*

> *25. As great crowds followed Jesus, He turned and said. 26. Anyone who follows Me cannot be My disciple unless he loves Me more than his father and mother, wife and children, brothers and sisters, yes and his own life also. 27. And whoever does not bear his own cross and follow Me, cannot be My disciple. (Luke 14:25-26 EDNT)*

EDUCATE COMMUNITY AND CHURCHGOERS THROUGH A LEARNING CENTRE APPROACH WITH OPEN-DOOR CLASSES.

4

MATURE Constituency Through Open-Door Study Classes

– making biblical discipleship a core learning experience together with relevant textbook studies to equip community and church families to become problem-solvers and effective servant leaders.

An Open-Door Policy

An open-door policy for study classes would be to invite all interested parties to attend and communicate to churchgoers and the community that they were welcome to participate. An objective is to allow a free exchange of ideas between church and community. The class leader encourages openness and transparency with all who attended. The objective is to stimulate interest in the subject matter, arouse a spirit of inquiry, and get the church and community involved in the process of learning and using all information gained in class.

The outcome would be to develop missional discipleship to benefit individuals and families and equip believers to become both social and spiritual problem solvers in their area of influence. Hopefully, those who study in a learning center environment would be effective and efficient servant leaders and become adequately equipped for hands-on community service and user-friendly ministry in the constituency of the church-at-large. A primary objective is to mature believers into missional disciples.

Marks of Maturity

Maturing believers will mellow, season, and become more Christ-like in their behavior as they grow in grace and knowledge. This is based on slow and careful growth. The work of teachers, mentors and spiritual coaches is to watch for these seven (7) behaviors that mark movement toward maturity:

1. Seriously keeps appointments and commitments
2. Remaining stable when praised or criticized
3. Maintaining a spirit of humility and tolerance
4. Making decisions with integrity and grace
5. Behaving with appreciation and gratitude
6. Affirming others before themselves
7. Walking honestly before others as a witness

Guide for Mentors and Coaches

2. We always give thanks to God for you all, without ceasing making mention of you in our intercessory prayers; 3. Remembering your faith that produced works, and love that prompted labor, and hope in the Lord Jesus Christ that brought about endurance before God and our Father; 4. knowing beloved that you have been chosen of God. 5. For our good news came not only in human speech, but also in words with innate power, and in the Holy Spirit, and crammed full of conviction, as you know what kind of leaders we were among you for your sake. (1 Thessalonians 1:2-5 EDNT)

Those who handle the Word need Spiritual Guidance *12. I have many more things to say to you, but you are not strong enough for them now. 13. However,* **when the Spirit of the Truth comes, He will guide you into all truth:** *The Spirit will not speak from Himself; but whatever He hears, that shall He speak: and He will show you future things.* **14. He shall honor Me: for He will receive out of My essence and will reveal this to you. 15. All things that the Father has are mine: therefore, the Spirit will take of My essence and reveal it to you.** *(John 15:6-15 EDNT)*

Sunday School is a Misnomer

Sunday school was a misleading term because it was not a school on Sunday; it was given an inaccurate designation. In fact, Sunday school was more a social gathering of friends for fellowship than a place to study and learn. To be a school there had to be teaching and learning. This required leaders, curriculum, guidance, study, teaching, and students engaged in a learning process. Instead the Sunday activity was normally a social event and there was little or no actually learning. In fact, research comparing those who attended Sunday school for twenty years and those who had never attended, discovered that those who had never attended scored as high on Bible content exams. The class structure on Sunday failed to meet the basic criteria for Christian education.

Yet, when Bible History Programs are permitted in a public school systems, based on pre and post-tests, 85% increase in bible content knowledge. This has been validated by the Hamilton County Public Schools' Bible History Program in Chattanooga, Tennessee. In this limited time and secular classroom, students learned Bible Content. Why doesn't the church accomplish similar results? What was the difference: competent and consistent instruction in a teaching/learning environment? It is tragic that public schools can do a better job of teaching biblical content than local churches.

> ***Word was not Woven into their Lives*** *1. Let us be on guard, while the promise of entering His rest still holds; that none of you may be found to be delinquent and come up short. 2. The good news was proclaimed to us, as well as to them:* ***but the word was not heard and therefore did not profit them, because it was not woven into the fabric of their faith when it was spoken.*** *3. This rest is only to be attained by those who have* ***learned to believe****; (Hebrews 4:1-3a EDNT*

On dealing with this problem in a graduate course on how to integrate knowledge learned in higher education into the operation of spiritual instruction, a public school teacher was asked how her church divided children on Sunday. Her answer was "*By age.*" When pressed if that were the best way, her answer was *"No, I am a reading teacher, children should be tested to determine their reading level and placed with others at the same level, so they could learn."* This was a shock to several church leaders in the class, but it clearly explained that educated members of the church, who knew the teaching and learning process were normally silent about the failure of Sunday school to fulfill an adequate role in educating the young in Bible content.

No Informed Participants

There were no students with advance study to prepare them to become an informed participant in class and no homework to guide their study. It was a social event for fellowship similar to a small gathering of family and friends. The program appeared to be similar to a small service before the morning church service. Often there were songs, prayer requests, a prayer, plans for the next class party, an offering, news about birthdays, baby showers. weddings and funerals. And of course, details about the sick and dying and particulars about their demise and of course gifts needed for the flower fund. In the adult classes, there was often a kind of "organ recital" about all the operations everybody had endured or was about to suffer. If there were time left before the bell, a little talk about the lesson may occur. However, there was little interest in the lesson and almost no preparation by the teacher. Class members did not come prepared to participate as a learner. They were just waiting for someone to ring the bell. It was not a class, but a social event called Sunday school. Some years ago, a national magazine called this the *"most wasted hour of the week."* Notwithstanding, this judgment, the church did little to improve the learning environment.

What was missing was an organized class structure that was designed both to teach Bible content and special textbook courses on subjects of interest with content that was needed by the churchgoers. There were no "Antioch-type Teaching" efforts similar to Saul and Barnabas who for "one whole year" (365 days) taught converts before the public recognized students as disciples as being Faith-based learners (Acts 11:19—30). At Antioch it was the secular merchants who recognized that these disciples transacted their business in a Messiah-like manner. There must be systematic teaching for new converts and structured guidance for discipleship. There were no lessons on family life, family budget, raising children, spiritual outreach to the community; there were no scheduled community and family involvement in the process of education.

What was missing was the CLASS division in the Celebration, Congregation, Class, and Cell structure that grows and develops faith-based constituencies into learning centers that could change the world. This lack was in spite of Biblical content that clearly taught that all officers and leaders of the church were to be "**apt to teach.**" Paul's benchmark instruction about leaders being able to teach clearly shows that those who have the responsibility of being learning leaders must have the ability to communicate and apply the truth of scripture with clarity and reason. This ability is not limited to those who speak from the pulpit, but all involved in spiritual leadership must be "*apt (able) to teach.*" The ability to teach is considered by some to be a spiritual gift and to others a learned behavior. Regardless, sacred scripture is clear: **teachers must teach!**

Danger of Being a Teacher

1. Do not be too eager, my cherished band of believers, to impart instruction to others; be certain that, if you do, you will be called to account more strictly. 2. There are many faults in us; but if a man never loses his language footing, he is a man completely able to keep the whole body under control. (James 3:1-2 EDNT)

Criterion for Spiritual Leadership

2. One holding an office of watchful care must be scrupulous, faithful to a certain woman, watchful, sensible, orderly, hospitable, **experienced in teaching***; 3. neither intemperate, nor quarrelsome, free from the love of money; but gentle, not contentious, not a craving for possessions; 4. he must be one who is a good head of his own family and keeps his children in order by winning their full respect; 5. if a man has not learned how to manage his own household, will he know how to govern God's church? 6. Not a recent convert, lest being puffed up he fall into judgment of the devil. 7. Moreover he must have a good report from those outside the church; that he not fall into reproach and into the snare of the devil. (1 Timothy 3:1-7 EDNT)*

Concentrate on Teaching

<u>*I implore you, brethren, by the compassions of God that you place yourselves as a living sacrifice, consecrated and pleasing to God, which is your reasonable worship.*</u> *2. And be not fashioned according to this age: but* **be transformed by a new mental attitude, that you may confirm for your-selves what is good, acceptable, and the complete will of**

God. *3. For I say this through the grace given unto me, to every man that is among you, not to be high-minded more than he ought to be minded; but to **be sober-minded, according to the measure of faith God has given**. 4. For as the human body has many parts, and all parts do not have the same function: 5. so we, being many form one body in Christ, and **each one is mutually dependent on another. 6. Having gifts that differ according to the grace given to us;** if your gift is inspired speech, practice according to your proportion of faith; 7. **If your gift is serving others, minister well: and the teacher concentrate on teaching**; 8. the one who exhorts, must give attention to consolation; he who gives food, clothing or shelter for the poor, let it be done with no partiality; he that governs must do it with diligence; the one who shows compassion must do it with cheerfulness.* (Romans 12:1-8 EDNT)

CLASS (Infinity #)
Discipleship and Lifestyle Training

Class is best understood as regular study groups who meet to learn Bible content, knowledge of Christian discipleship, and facts about a missional lifestyle that will improve believers, enhance families, and encourage spiritual involvement in lifestyle propagation of the message of grace. A class is of indefinite size but must be populated by individuals interested in the subject at hand. Local leaders should remember that in Acts 11 it took Saul and Barnabas *"one whole year"* daily teaching converts before their lifestyle was recognized by a secular community. That was 365 days; not just an hour a week. A study group requires a learning leader, a teacher/coach/mentor to provide guidance for an informed discussion. Individuals in the class must do advance study to become an informed participant to create a learning environment required for individuals. This creates collective growth of the congregation. Understanding and following the classic principles of teaching will enhance the learning experience. The end is worth the journey, but some are not willing to walk the pathway that prepares them for biblical instruction because it may expose their personal lifestyle. Preparing to teach requires patience, persistence, prayerful concentration, and systematic study. All who prepare to teach must find a quiet and restful place to study.

Come Apart and Rest or Come Apart

30. And the apostles gathered themselves together with Jesus, and reported to Him all things, both what they had done, and what they had taught. 31 And He said to them, **Come apart to a quiet place and rest a while:** *for many were coming and going, and* **they had no time even to eat.** *32. And* **they departed secretly in a boat to a secluded place**. *(Mark 6:30-32 EDNT)*

Principles of Teaching

The teaching/learning process is central to the Class structure of the Congregation. In 1846 John Milton Gregory gave up the study of law to become a Baptist minister and a college professor, then an administrator, working primarily in Michigan and Illinois, where he organized the University of Illinois. Gregory was buried on the university campus in 1898, but his Seven **Laws of Teaching** survived and have been a blessing to many since they were clearly expressed in his book by that title published in 1884. These were timeless insights that remain useful. One who understands these basic rules will receive the praise of grateful students and will be honoring the Word that requires all leaders to be "apt to teach."

Neglect these fundamentals and teaching credentials and even subject-specific certification will be useless pieces of paper. Those who attempt to teach without Gregory's perspective will become frustrated and produce a class of passive and even resistant pupils. What does "pupil" mean? From the *Latin*, it describes a "little boy or doll." It suggests immaturity and the need for leadership. Teachers who do not effectively teach contribute to the immaturity of a generation and may be responsible for many of the problems that society and religion has to face because of unformed judgment and acts of undisciplined behavior. In the simplest form, the Laws of Teaching are still relevant to the needs of learners and can be a blessing to faith-based instruction. The Seven *Laws of Teaching* written by Professor Gregory should be learned and practiced by all who wish to teach others:

1. **The teacher must know that which he or she would teach.**
2. **A learner must attend with interest to the lesson being taught.**
3. **The language, used as a medium between teacher and learner, must be common to both.**

4. **The facts to be taught must be learned through facts already known.**
5. **Excite and direct the self-activity of the learner, as a rule telling them nothing they can learn on their own.**
6. **The learner must reproduce in his or her own words the facts to be learned.** Memorization is the first level of learning. After the facts of the lesson are clear there is an elementary degree of understanding. The next step in the process is the ability to paraphrase a thought or concept in one's own words. Finally, the desire to initiate a search for supportive evidence to reinforce one's understanding is realized and an effort made to apply what was learned. Application is required to reinforce the learning process.
7. **At least one-third of teaching/study/class time should be given to review and/or application of the lessons learned.**

A restatement of these laws:

1. The learning leader/coach/mentor must know the subject.
2. A learner is one who attends with interest to the lesson.
3. The language, used as a medium between teacher and learner, must be common to both.
4. The facts to be taught must be learned through facts already known.
5. Excite and direct the self-motivation of learners, as a rule telling them nothing they can learn on their own.

6. The learner must reproduce in his or her own words the facts to be learned.

   (a) **Memorization** is the first level of learning.

   (b) After the facts of the lesson are clear there is an elementary degree of **understanding**.

   (c) The next step in the process is the ability to **paraphrase** a thought or concept in one's own words.

   (d) Finally the desire to search for **supportive evidence** to support one's understanding is realized and an effort made to apply what was learned.

   (e) **Application** is required to reinforce the learning process.

   Summary:
   - What does the lesson say?
   - What does the lesson mean?
   - How can I express the meaning in my own words?
   - How can I verify that my understanding is acceptable?
   - How can I apply the lesson to my life and the present situation of others?

7. At least one-third of teaching/study/class time should be given to review and/or application of the data to be learned.

Inductive or Self-Study

Inductive study, at times understood to be self-study, is a method-based path to learning. Method is based on the Greek word *methodos,* which literally means a way or path of transit. Method implies orderly, logical, and effective arrangement and may denote either an abstraction or a concrete procedure. Method is a way of doing things, which carefully maintains and fosters conditions conducive to understanding and growth.

Inductive or self-study is where an individual follows a specific plan to better understand what the author means by the words written and the way the words are put together.   One may better interpret what is written by following the procedure self-evident in the seven words or constructs below.

This hermeneutical process is systematic and rewarding:

1. **See** - observe the link between subject and object.
2. **Inquire** - inquisitiveness is required to find the meaning.
3. **Answer** - re-creating the attitude or intent of the writer is a source of answers.
4. **Summarize** - integrate and summarize to discover message.
5. **Evaluate** - determine the local or universal value of what is written.
6. **Apply** – a universal or specific application of the facts presented.
7. **Associate** - written passages must be associated with each other and with extra-source data to develop the ultimate correlation.

Create an open door to the community through community and family education.
(C.A.F.E.)

> Whom God calls, He qualifies, but God depends on others to teach and adequately prepare each one for their God given task. This includes a missional lifestyle and faith-based, biblical knowledge.

5

INCREASE The Care Of Souls In Cells

— maturing believers in small groups invested with the cure/care of souls through faith, spiritual nourishment, friendship, and fellowship.

An early task for the spiritual leader is to guide new believers into informal associations and personal involvement with a cohort of like-minded individuals and scheduled informal activities on the church calendar. Cells are designed to make biblical discipleship a core learning experience for maturating of believers. Do not start with teaching doctrine or rules of conduct, give the new people time to grow in grace before they are introduced to the formal aspects of organized religion. Unless the new person begins to feel a part of what is going on they will quickly withdraw.

Friends and activities that interest the person should be a priority. The spiritual leader should make a strong effort to introduce the new convert to individuals, programs, and activities that would be beneficial and easy participation. For example, if a new person is placed in an advanced Bible study class without a working knowledge of what is being studied, they may feel overwhelmed and easily become discouraged. This is why a "new converts class" is a good place to start with a good teacher who can assist in a basic understanding and initiate the foundation stones for their path forward to discipleship and spiritual participation in the life of the church. When new folk do not find a place that feels like home they will be lost to the group.

Evangelism, Disciple Making and Soul Care

Cell is a small group of (8-12) individuals who meet regularly for prayer and sharing. Small groups individuals known as Cells, actually serve the congregation and community through their collective efforts; which include the personal care and cure of souls, expansion and growth in both influence and numbers, a spiritual ministry that changes lives, consistent nurture for new believers, broaden the leadership base through volunteerism, assist with congregational extension and church planting. This is all done through a missional lifestyle, working together in harmony, and walking daily in fellowship with the Lord and other believers.

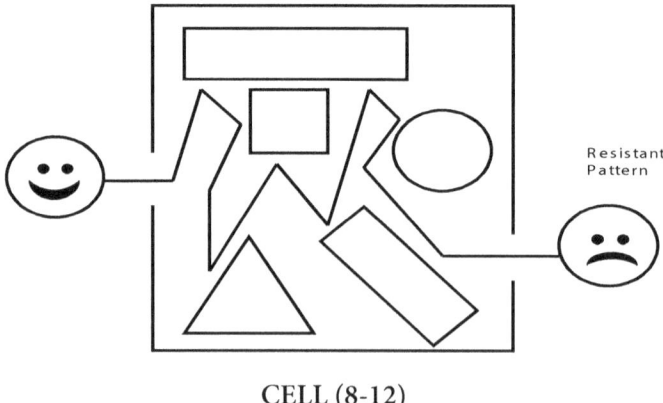

CELL (8-12)

Small groups of committed believers meeting regularly for discussions about evangelism can enable individuals to become soul winners. Prospective converts may be invited to the session for exposure to serious believers. Potentially weak constituents may become a part to gain stamina and strength for the journey. Such missional lifestyle examples work in a complicated and confused world, but it must be regularly encouraged through prayer and fellowship. Perhaps the church should replace their committees by Cell-type groups designated as Action Groups with special agendas for advancing the kingdom. Cell groups are the nucleus or heart of the congregation. They serve God as a family through fellowship, praise and worship. They minister to each other through Scripture, spiritual gifts, practical help, by coaching and mentoring for disciple making. They reach the community through a missional lifestyle, verbal witness, both active and passive.

Some mature Cell groups can become Action Groups to work with the pastor with assigned agendas to bring renewal and more active participation in scheduled activities. Active cell groups can grow into an Alliance for Evangelism and become a major asset for the leadership staff in handling the extensive work of a local congregation. Most faith-based groups suffer from lack of leadership and individuals in service groups. Select groups from working cells could easily become Action Groups for the Alliance for Evangelism.

Alliance For Evangelism

Action Groups are small groups of seven (7) active people working with the Pastor to bring program elements up from the people, encourage creative thinking through barnstorming sessions, and restore energy, conviction, and commitment to improve participation in all aspects of church life. This is a special use of the Cell or small group concept in addition to the regular mission of the Cell ministry in the care and cure of souls. Each Action Group has a Leader and a Secretary and five (5) members; that is seven clusters of seven working with the Pastor. Forty-nine additional people working on the special needs of the gathered church. This can make a difference in evangelism, outreach, watch care, and renewal.

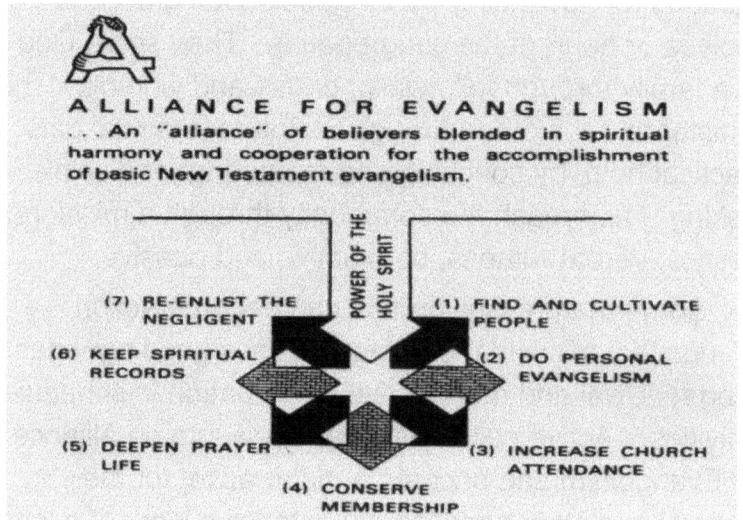

Building Interactive Connection

Cells build relationships for the cure and care of souls. Working cell groups become a subdivision of the watch care for new and growing disciples. Mature leadership is required to lead these specialized groups, called cells. All living things grow by cell enlargement and cell division. Cell groups are a basic element of

Kingdom Growth Through Missional Lifestyle. These interactive connections create contacts for evangelism and discipleship. Anytime an unconverted individual makes it to the sanctuary unsaved it is clear evident the local program of evangelism is not working. Anytime active members become discouraged it is evidence that the care of souls is not adequately working. True evangelism is reaching the lost at their point of need at the earliest time and at the farthest distance from the sanctuary of the church.

Prevention of discouragement and drop out of members from the congregation is to anticipate their needs before it becomes a problem. This is where spiritual discernment and leadership becomes active in the watch care of the congregation. Fellowship is the function of a missional lifestyle that finds and cultivates individuals and presents solutions to spiritual problems before they happen. The good news of salvation is made available to uninformed individuals that leads to a conversion experience. Spiritual watch care is available to maintain each congregant at a spiritual level sufficient to maintain a worthy lifestyle. The converts and new members are brought into the assembly for identification with the Trinity through Baptism and/or to receive scriptural instruction in lifestyle as presented in the Word of God. Cell groups assist the class structure and the leadership in doing some of this primary work.

Through the process of mentoring, coaching, teaching, loving, and sharing friendship, cell groups assist with making kingdom disciples not necessarily adding members to the local church. Souls must be won without the idea of building attendance; true converts will find a scriptural place of worship where they have friend and neighbors. Cell groups create an atmosphere for growth and congregational growth takes place as a by-product of a missional lifestyle.

Fruit is on New Growth

Fruit is always on new growth and personal evangelism is done best by new converts. New converts are prepared for the witness to others by caring believers. A new converts has within their acquaintance and friendship about 200 contacts: this is the potential for fruitful outreach and must be executed by a "first generation enthusiasm" of new folk. Fruit is always on new growth. According to Genesis "the seed is in the fruit"; consequently, individual converts must be guided to share with family and friends what God has done in their lives. This can be done as they grow in grace and knowledge and become an active disciple learning more of Christ to be effective as a messenger a "sent one" sharing salvation with others. Thus, becoming a witness, a believer develops a lifestyle. Witness comes from the word *martyr* "willing to suffer for a cause." Martyrs of the past were not *martyrs* because they died for their faith; they died for their faith because they lived their faith and were true witnesses or *martyrs* to the end.

Expansion of the Kingdom

True celebration and worship directed toward God and fellowship within a like-minded congregation advances expansion of the kingdom through evangelism. One becomes two; two becomes four; four become sixteen: this is exponential growth. In spiritual development, there is an exponential function: the exponent is the work of the Holy Spirit in the life and witness of individual believers supported by a missional congregation. There is no substitute for personal lifestyle in winning souls. Paul further challenged these new converts to a missional lifestyle:

> **20. Now seeing we are representatives for Christ, as though God did make His appeal through us: we implore you in Christ's stead, come together with God. 21. For God caused Christ to become sin for us, who knew no sin; that we might come into right standing with God in Christ.** *(2 Corinthians 5:20-21 EDNT)*

The normal growth of living things is perpetuated by cell enlargement and cell division, but the process does not always work effectively or efficiently. There is not always a readiness to grow or the resources to grow normally. In the scientific study of plants there are differences as individual plants adjust to the soil and the environment. In biology one deals with the science of all forms of life, including their classification, physiology, chemistry, and interactions. This study is concerned with living organisms, their structure, function, growth, origin, abnormalities over time, and reproduction. Abnormalities include size, number, shape, color, and miscellaneous anomalies. The study of plant life includes vitality, survival, and reproductive strength.

In the study of Miller's Living Systems, all living things share commonalities of a specific origin, a pattern of developmental growth, viability, and decline and death. According to Miller, organisms, organizations, and organizations share a similar process. Since the church is considered a social institution, a local church or a collection of churches, would share a similar life-span process. One thing is certain: the process of growth is dynamic, and the phases or stage normally relate to the strengthening of the unit for viability and reproduction rather than being related to size.

Some years ago, while speaking at a Canadian Church Growth Conference a discussion was created about the size of local churches. In reviewing the concept of growth someone suggested that this view depreciated the large super-church in favor of the small community congregation. The question was asked, *"How large should a church be?"* The response was, *"How large should a cow be?"* The questioner answered that he did not know.

The group was asked if they were required to determine the normal size of a cow, how they would go about the process. It was suggested that perhaps one should observe and count some cows to determine the average or normal size. The apparent answer was that most mature cows were about the same size.

The next question was, *"What if you owned a cattle ranch and discovered a cow in the pasture that was 25 times larger than all the other cows, what would you do?"* A participant answered, *"I would get it out of the pasture as quickly as possible before it stepped on some other cows."*

Could this have relevance for the mega-church? If not in the process of becoming an abnormally large church, then soon after other smaller congregations in the area may be trampled. This is not the intention of church leadership, but is a logical consequence of supergrowth. Everyone wants their church to grow, but normal growth should have some relevance to evangelism of the local community; not just collecting strays and dropouts from declining assemblies.

This fact exists. Research demonstrated that in one southern city a large Baptistic congregation brought about the demise of thirteen other small Baptist churches. It is the law of the sea: big fish eat little fish. Notwithstanding, the church needs to be large enough to support an effective ministry to a community, the data suggests that small congregations are generally more effective in evangelism and missions. A few mega churches scattered around the United States will not adequately serve the spiritual needs of thousands of cities and communities. Small churches must be encouraged to go and plant other churches, but stay in the community and serve. The motto should be: "**Go and grow; stay and serve!**"

What size can the community support without doing harm to other faith-based groups? Perhaps we should remember the words of Jesus in Mark 9:36-40:

> *36. And Jesus took a little child, and placed him among them: and when He had taken him in His arms, He said, 37. Whoever receives (for themselves) little children in my name, receives Me: and whoever shall receive Me, receives not me alone, but Him who sent Me. 38. And John said, Master, we saw one casting out devils using your name, and we forcefully told him to stop, because he does not follow us. 39. But Jesus said, Do not hinder him: for there is no man who will do a mighty works in My name,*

who can quickly speak evil of Me. 40. For whoever is not against us is on our side

It should be remembered that kingdom growth is based on two factors: new converts and new congregations. Gathering members from other churches is attendance building not true kingdom growth, academically it is called "transfer growth" but in reality it is not growth of the kingdom. Each growing church should evaluate the "nature" of their growth and be certain that in their zeal to build attendance they are not causing others to suffer loss. Check information about the problems of growth measured by the relationship formula in Chapter Three; it is [R = *n x (n-1)*]; in words <u>*[number - times (number -- minus one) equals number of interactions and/or interpersonal relationships]*.</u>

A Self-defeating Theology

A change in the KJV translation that made a difference were the words in Matthew (28:19, 20) *19. Go ye therefore, and teach all nations, baptizing them in the name of the Father, and of the Son, and of the Holy Ghost: 20. Teaching them to observe all things whatsoever I have commanded you: and, lo, I am with you always, even unto the end of the world. Amen.* (KJV)

A Fresh Consideration

A fresh consideration for the primary command of the verse translated "teach" would provide a clear understanding: the Greek word used was *matheteuo,* to *instruct with the purpose of making a disciple; the word suggested not only to learn but to be attached to and become a follower of the teacher.* Greek words have special designations, *matheteuo* here was classified as *aorist imperative active* which denotes a command, or entreaty and indicates the action as being accomplished by the subject of the verb. Later versions translated the word as "make disciples" which was better. Yet, in most translations the participle "going" remains an imperative "go." This makes the words of Jesus a theology of coercion in an effort to compel followers to "go and do" instead of "do as they go." This was not a Commission for the Church, but a plan of action for all believers as they daily traveled. This was a Believers Challenge to a missional ministry of discipleship. They were to make disciples as they spread the Gospel by the process of disciple making through conversion, the sacrament of Identification with the Godhead, and equipping converts with all the instructions of Jesus. The following paragraphs make the intention of Challenge of Jesus clear.

The Challenge of Jesus

The main problem with the translation of Jesus' Challenge is that it was not given as a Commission to an established or organized assembly, but given to the close followers of Jesus as personal guidance. Another basic problem relates to the three participles: Go [*going* or as you go] ... *baptizing* ... *teaching* --each participles dependent upon the main verb *teach* translated "make disciples." Although such a verbal construction was not uncommon for the participles themselves to assume the force of a weak imperative, similar to the indirect command in modern English, i.e. "**As you go, close the door**!" However, the command "*make disciples*" is the primary command, while the participles served as weak commands: **going, baptizing** and *teaching* as ways of fulfilling the primary mission made implicit by the challenge of Jesus. The concept of *"as you go"* was clearly understood by those who heard His words.

A Participle is not an Imperative

Some academics translate one of three Greek participles, *going or as you go,* as an imperative, a command. This places a different emphasis on the words of Jesus and creates a theology of coercion not intended. The only imperative was *"teach/make disciples"* of all four verb forms, *"Going ... make disciples ... baptizing ... teaching"* (but the King James translators chose to make "go" and "teach/make disciples" direct commands, but not *baptizing* and *teaching*. One should either make all the participles into weak commands or leave the verb form as participles as originally written.

What difference does this make?

The above translation created a self-defeating theology of coercion in an effort to compel people to *"go and do"* rather that establish a *"do as you go"* missional lifestyle. Also, organized leadership spend inordinate energy in the ***"go and do"*** and little effort in teaching believers to observe all things that Jesus directed, and this included an identification of all learners with the full work of the Trinity as a part of baptism. This is why converts are baptized in the *"Name (authority) of the Father, the Son, and the Holy Spirit."*

Water Baptism Instruction is Incomplete

When water baptism becomes a one-time rite for others to watch without the Candidate being taught that Baptist is to be identified with the role of the Trinity in their life, the Candidate has been short-changed and will demonstrate a weak understanding and have less value of Holy Communion and other ceremonies designed to keep a believer current in their relationship with God; such as, freely giving, worship participation, using their time, talent, and resources for advancing the kingdom, ongoing fellowship, and outreach efforts for the cure of souls. Since Water Baptism and Holy Communion are two significant sacraments instituted by Jesus, Candidates are not prepared to take on a mature missional lifestyle and true worship without full involvement of the Trinity in their daily lives and public worship.

The Great Commission was not a command for the church to "go," but a challenge to a missional lifestyle for people already in the process of going into the known world to carry the good news. They were instructed to wait for the power of the Spirit. It was guidance to effectively follow-up those who received the teaching, embraced the teacher, and became an active learner. Why would scholars make such a decision that changed the meaning of the words of Jesus? All academics and theologians are influence by an intellectual and cultural bias that takes years and firm methodology to control.

6

EDUCATE Community And Churchgoers Through A Learning Centre Ministry

— a moral and intellectual effort to equip believers to become problem-solvers and effective servant leaders to advance the gospel.

A local congregation must be a "learning centre" before the membership and worshipers develop a missional lifestyle. A biblical foundation in scriptural content is necessary to support a relational congregation and a missional lifestyle for believers. The class structure and curriculum for study should reflect an open-door outreach which teaches the true meaning of scripture and textbook courses of interest and value to the church family and the community.   It is recommended to use the C.A.F.E. Edition of the EVERGREEN Devotional New Testament for bible content and textbook courses from Alpha Institute of Ministry (**A.I.M.) supplemented by textbooks chosen by local leaders.**

Become a Wholesome Teacher

*1. But you must speak those things that are appropriate for **healthy teaching**: 2. Charge the **senior men** to be sober, serious, prudent, healthy in Christian faith and love and* *endurance. 3. The* **senior women** *likewise must behave appropriately for a holy calling, not given to slanderous talk or given to wine, teaching others by good example: 4. in order* <u>**that they may train the young women** to be lovers of their husbands and child lovers, 5. to be sensible, pure, homemakers, good, lining up under the authority of their husbands lest the word of God be abused with foul language. 6. The **younger men** similarly exhort to be sensible, 7. about all things,</u> **showing yourself a pattern of good works in your teaching display purity of motive and seriousness. 8. Present a wholesome message that cannot be criticized**; *in this way your opponents may be ashamed, having nothing disparaging to say to you. 9. Encourage servants to line up under the authority of their masters and comply with their instructions; not being contentious; 10. not embezzling but* **showing loyalty and faithfulness;** *that they may beautify the teaching of God our Savior in all things.* (Titus 2:1-10 EDNT)

THE LEARNING CENTRE PROJECT FOR FAITH-BASED GROUPS

*"***H**elping **E**veryone **L**earn **P**roficiently*"*

Available options with qualified teachers, certificates of completion and participation honors.

THE LEARNING CENTRE is a not-for-profit venture to extend the Faith-based ministry of local churches and missionary endeavors to extend their teaching ministry to beyond the local congregation.

THE LEARNING CENTRE has several options but may be operated as separate programs or a comprehensive unit for a Christian educational program under **THE LEARNING CENTRE** and Alpha Institute of Ministry **(A.I.M.)** with the **ACADEMY** (k-12) Division for Primary and Secondary children or the alternative delivery student assistance programs, **C.A.F.E.** being a Division for **A.I.M.** for Bible content and leadership training of the local congregation. Community service and practical ministry to the community and the local Sunday school and youth classes for discipleship and ministry training are related to **C.A.F.E. / A.I.M.** being the post-secondary Division to train youth and adult believers studying for lifestyle witness, church leadership, missional training, community service and practical ministry. In this delivery system, teachers and assistants may function, presenting the same textbook subject or the Scriptural Content in **The EVERGREEN Devotional New Testament** at different times and at different levels. This concept is a comprehensive Bible content training program for local faith-based groups that also serves the community, other area faith-based groups or other local churches. EVERGREEN furnishes weekly study for a four-year curriculum covering the complete New Testament.

The **LEARNING CENTRE** logo represents integration of the church and community which is the comprehensive logo for all the listed programs and options. All faith-based congregations can work together to reach the community and families with basic

Christianity to show *pure religion" in the community. The psychology of color shows that black and white have many meanings; however, the colors can also symbolize the starkness of decision-making when one is confronted with during hard *choices.

The Learning Centre Logo

The Squares are black and white and have four equal sides and four right angles. The four sides represent equality: personal, social, spiritual and racial. The center square represents structured or established congregations working together in fellowship to advance commonalities of religious faith. It is common ground, not differences, that advance knowledge and understanding. An X is interwoven with the center square representing the church and with itself representing the integration of basic Christianity. The

X-shaped cross, commonly called the St. Andrew's Cross, was named for Simon Peter's brother, Andrew, who was martyred by crucifixion on an X-shaped cross at his own request, because he deemed himself unworthy to be crucified in the same manner as Jesus. The X-shaped cross signifies his resolution or resolve.

The fish symbol occurred early in Christian history and was placed in the center of the cross. After the crucifixion believers were persecuted and the fish became a symbol Christians would recognize, but others would not. Therefore, believers could connect through this symbol without being exposed to their oppressors. The Greek word for fish, IXΘYΣ, was used as an acrostic to advance the Christian faith. The Greek letters for fish were given the meaning "Jesus Christ God's Son Savior" to the early believers. They also saw the X-shaped cross in the tail of the fish. The FISH symbol was placed in the center of the cross to represent a central concept of a common faith in Jesus Christ.

OPTIONS

(1)
THE ACADEMY
(K-12) or K-3; K-6; K-9; K-12; or Academic Performance Training Students
A.P.T.S.

"Helping Every-age Learn Proficiently"

Can you imagine a place where learning differences are a testimony to God's creativity? Can you envision a learning center where children can thrive educationally and develop a love for learning in a safe and caring environment? If you have been searching for an answer to your child's special needs or looking for a school where teachers care for the heart and soul of each student, the Academy may be the answer.

It is not too late, if your son or daughter is struggling in the present learning environment and needs an affordable, specialized learning atmosphere that serves students of all ages regardless of learning difficulties or those simply struggling in school. The Academy will test and evaluate each child and based on an academic and psychological assessment, design a way forward for a significant learning experience.

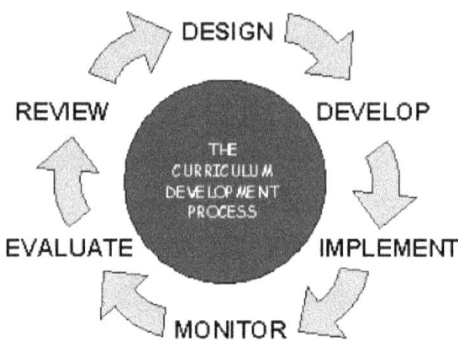

The Curriculum Development Process

The Learning Centre — Academy division is a comprehensive class-based school using a Classical K-12 Grammar School concept with many options. The Academy can be a full (K-12) classroom school; an Internet or Skype delivery system; a Home School support model; or a phased-in model beginning at Primary level age 4-12 and growing to the Secondary level for ages 11-18. The curriculum providing age-appropriate information is only part of the reason students perform well; adapting studies to individual learning styles by teachers with a heart for children is what makes the difference. Most class-rooms attempt a one size fits all, but every child learns in his/her own way.

The Academy creates a specialized class-room with an effective learning option personalized to meet the needs of each child. The Academy will assist you to find out why your child is not learning. Can you conceive of a brighter, happier, and more confident child? The Academy tests and customizes the learning experience to the unique abilities of each student. This creates the ideal opportunity for students to learn and excel.

Teaching that is tailored for each student means less stress and more learning, based on a faculty concept the Academy called **SCAN – Student Concerns Are Normalized** through testing and evaluation. The Academy gives parents a choice with curriculum divided into age-level needs. The age ranges specify the youngest age for a child entering that year and the oldest age for a child leaving that year. An understanding of the dynamic process of change, growth and interaction in the classroom will assist the teacher in dealing with attentiveness and productivity.

A primary task of the teacher is control of the classroom in order to direct the energy of each student in the discovery of the essential elements of the core content covered in the session. It is beneficial to remember that content is not an end in itself; it is a vehicle to transport the student through the learning process. Based on the maturity of the students involved, interaction between students limits their ability to look at and pay attention to the teacher. When this becomes obvious, the teacher feels undervalued and this further limits learning. An understanding of this process will assist the teacher in special preparation to maintain the interest, curiosity, and efficiency of the student. Efficiency in learning would mean productivity without loss or waste by each student in the class. The goal is to make each student a moral citizen of society before they can become a mystical citizen of heaven.

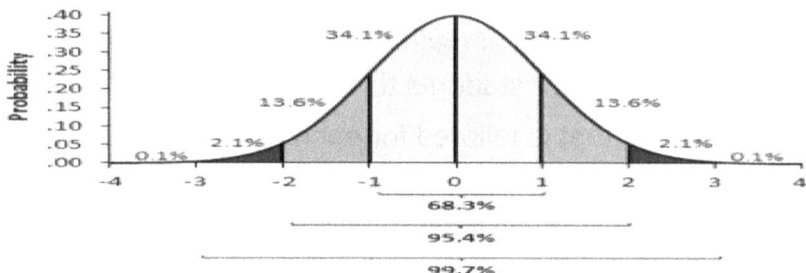

Obstinate Learners	Reluctant Learners	Informal Learners	Excellent Learners
Are unwilling to change and difficult to manage	Are cautious about participating, but will follow the crowd	Require a more relaxed, less structured process	Have a strong desire to learn

Student Attitudes or Predisposition to Learn.

Healthy age-specific development together with positive influence from family and friends will produce an excellent student who desires to learn. Teaching such students is almost effortless because they are self-starters. The development of certain personality traits and individual characteristics may produce an informal learner who requires a more relaxed and less structured process for learning. Such students may see things differently than others and develop study and work habits that may not fit the norm. In reality, these students may not receive the highest grades in the class, but they may actually be the better learners with long-term benefits that predict personal and professional achievements.

In some educational systems, the informal learner may be classified as a "C" student but will probably end up owning the business and hiring the excellent "A" students to do the work. A list in history may verify this possibility. Some of the informal learners that ended up on top of the heap were Edison, Lincoln, Einstein, von Braun, Reagan, Kennedy, Clinton, Bush, and the list goes on and on.

The Academy will normally use the curriculum developed by the governmental entity of the state to prepare students to take the available standard exams and be prepared to seek higher placement. The difference is the quality of instruction and the supportive attitude of the leadership. If the Academy uses the same curriculum as the public schools, so what is the difference? The primary differences are:

1. All students are tested, assessed, and placed by a specialized system that assists the Academic in placing the student in the proper division and with the proper teacher.

2. Teacher attitudes and approach to individual students is based on the above assessment.

3. Students are grouped into a common classroom with a specialized teacher and a teaching assistant or teacher's aide.

4. No student feels classified or categorized in the group of students, but each work at their own pace guided by the faculty. One student may excel without another feeling left behind. Individual differences are handled one-on-one by the teacher and not as a class.

5. Students are permitted to advance at their own pace and may be moved to the next higher level class whenever the teacher feels they are ready to perform adequately at the next level. Advancement or promotion to the next level class is a judgment call of the present teacher. When "excellent" work at one level adequately predicts good performance at the next level, a student is advanced. Such "any time" advancement becomes an encouragement for others to excel.

6. All students are placed in one of three primary levels or one of three secondary levels. These levels are shown below and provide for a range of ages and academic levels to provide a "comfort index" in the affective domain and a "learning index" in the cognitive domain. This is the opposite of "main streaming" where individual students feel out of place; it clearly places a student in a learning group where they may receive individual attention and progress at their own pace.

7. The process creates a learning environment where individuals learn from each other and develop individual study skills and participate in group learning exercises. The grouping of the students is a specialized aspect of the Academy and is believed to be the basis for an excellent learning environment.

Difference is Primarily the Teacher

Learning in theory is both intellectual and rational. In reality, the educational process is a highly emotional and inter-personal practice and requires a combination of

intellectual excitement and interpersonal rapport. There must be an empathy relationship between teacher and learner. This is a trust relationship with firm reliance on the integrity and ability of the teacher and a concern for learning expressed by the student. The faculty directed learning model works only with integrity and trust.
(See APPENDIX for Primary and Secondary Age-level Divisions)

(2)

C.A.F.E.©
COMMUNITY AND FAMILY EDUCATION©

Providing Practical Bible Study, Lifestyle Training for Family Life, Community Service, and Faith-based lifestyle witnessing.

C.A.F.E. is designed as nourishment for mind, soul, and body. The **C.A.F.E.** logo represents the integration of Biblical study with growth and development classes within the church (the white square). The larger white square represents the community with **C.A.F.E.** reaching outside the four walls. The large black square represents the world in which the believers exist as a faith-based entity. Local Sunday school and Christian educational classes for youth training have suffered significant decline in recent decades, it is time for a new approach to community and family education. **C.A.F.E.** may be an answer to this uncertainty.

C.A.F.E is a 4-year program sponsored by a faith-based group to teach community service and practical ministry, through basic New Testament content and practical textbook courses in an informal setting. **C.A.F.E** may be used to replace the youth and adult aspects of local education by faith-based groups to better reach families and the community. Although classes will be a "colloquy"—a discussion rather than a taught class, student participation is the objective. Advance preparation each week by class members create a **C.A.F.E.** Class of informed participants ready to learn and share.

Enrollment and Classes

C.A.F.E. may be the answer to the decline in local Christian education and classes for youth training. it is time for a new approach to community and family education. Students will enroll for one year or one term at a time and renew the enrollment based on subject interest and participation. Award documentation of completion will be issued each year for those completing three Terms with a Qualification Credential after four years. **C.A.F.E.** is designed for attendees of the local fellowship and to reach families in the community. It will also develop leadership for the local assembly, strengthen families, and equip believers for faith-based lifestyle witness in the community. Students are enrolled and pay a small fee for books [new community people may receive a "visitor's scholarship" for the first term.] Those enrolled are assigned to read a section of a book or a passage of sacred scripture before coming to class and thereby become an informed participant in class discussion. *This has been a major weakness in Sunday* *school and youth classes; no one but the teacher makes any preparation.*

Each class has a leader or mentor (not a lecturer) to guide the discussion relative to the assigned reading. This is an active, participatory and integrated approach to faith-based education where all students feel they are part of the class and may make a contribution to the learning process. This is a significant step in advancing faith-based education. Also, research has shown that when individuals are "enrolled" they are more apt to attend class; when students make advance preparation, they are more likely to participate. When they pay a small "fee for textbooks, refreshments; etc." this improves both attendance and participation.

Cafe Atmosphere for Classes

C.A.F.E. is structured to be held in an informal setting; such as, a dining hall, or classroom arranged with tables. The first 15-minutes of class, students should be allowed to have fellowship and quietly eat a snack or drink to create the "cafe" atmosphere. This will accommodate those who travel a distance or miss a meal to participate. The informal setting should not be permitted to hinder the class discussion period. The leader should moderate an informal conversation based on the assigned reading and advance study. Questions and comments on the assigned reading should be welcomed and encouraged from all students. Discussion should be limited to the area of assigned reading or questions for clarification about material already covered. The leader should make a brief summary of the discussion at the close of the class and remind students of the next reading assignment and the value of participating in scheduled classes.

Optional Class Scheduling*

All classes are scheduled for one hour, broken down as 15 minutes for fellowship/food, [to create the **C.A.F.E** atmosphere] and 45 minutes for class discussion and participation in learning. Two-classes once a week (recommended options)

Sunday: replace SS am and Training Hour pm or offer multiple classes during am and/or pm.

Doing everything on Sunday has not worked well, **TRY...**

Two-day Schedule with one Class:
- Tuesday and Thursday
- Wednesday and Saturday
- Wednesday and Sunday

One-day Schedule with Two Classes:
- Two 1-hour classes back to back on one day or
- Saturday Only Schedule: Two 1-hour classes back-to-back on Saturday

A.I.M./C.A.F.E. Curriculum

An option:

Present Community and Family Education (C.A.F.E.) through A.I.M. –Alpha Institute of Ministry at times other than Sunday morning.

A four-year curriculum is provided to prepare young people for volunteerism and community Service with non-profits, NGO's and/or faith-based groups who work with children, at-risk-youth, and dysfunctional families. **A.I.M./C.A.F.E.** curriculum is also designed to develop leadership in the local church and is coached by local leaders. Although classes will be a "colloquy"—a discussion rather than a taught class, student participation is the objective. **A.I.M./C.A.F.E.** has proved to be an essential source of local educational advancement and adequate training to equip individuals for community and practical ministry inside and outside the church. [*www.globalaim.net*]

(3)

A.I.M. — ALPHA INSTITUTE OF MINISTRY

*"Be eager to present yourself approved to God,
a workman unashamed, cutting straight
the word of truth."*

(2 Timothy 2:15 EDNT)

Vision and Mission

Alpha Institute of Ministry (**A.I.M.**) was established to restore biblical subject matter to faith-based leadership and ministry by teaching basic Bible content as well as the essential elements of practical ministry, community service and leadership. The mission is to assist young people to become a *"burning and shining light"* to their generation by guiding them in: learning the foundational contents of the Bible; grasping the essentials of community service; and working with local churches and non-profits, and faith-based organizations in the advancement of both social and spiritual services to the family, the community and society.

A.I.M. is designed as nourishment for mind, soul, and body. The logo represents the integration of Biblical Study with growth and development classes within the church (the white square). The larger white square represents the community with reaching outside the four walls. The large black square represents the world in which the church exists as a faith-based entity. Sunday school and youth training have suffered significant decline in recent decades, it is time for a new approach to community and family education. **A.I.M.** is a 4-year program sponsored by a faith-based group to teach practical ministry, community service and basic New Testament content in an informal setting. **A.I.M.** may be used to replace the youth and adult aspects of education by faith-based groups to better reach families and the community.

The visionary leadership of the Alpha Institute of Ministry **A.I.M.** desires to restore biblical subject matter to Christian leadership and ministry by teaching basic Bible content as well as the essential elements of leadership and Christian service. The Institute's mission is to assist the brightest young men and women to become a "burning and shining light" to their generation. Since "alpha" is the brightest star in the constellation and ALPHA is also a biblical reference to Christ, the founders believe that the brightest young Christians should be the first to be trained in Christian service and practical ministry. This is to be done by: learning the foundational contents of the Bible; understanding the essentials of Christian service; and working with local churches and non-profit, faith-based organizations in the advancement of both social and spiritual services to the family, the church and the community.

Complement not Compete

The primary objective of **A.I.M.** is to complement, and not to compete with, existing local church training programs and educational institutions that train individuals for Pastoral Ministry. **A.I.M.** should be seen as an "alpha" institution which recruits young Christians and new converts in order to initiate their preparation for the Christian service and practical ministry that is the call and obligation of every convert to Christianity. It is hoped that **A.I.M.** will be able to prepare students to become workers in the local church and to assist those who feel the call to general ministry to transfer credits earned at AIM to a degree granting institution for further education. In this regard, the founders of AIM see the program of study as a "feeder" and "recruiter" for established institutions that can further equip students for Pastoral or Missionary Service.

Curriculum Delivery Strategy

The Institute offers a Course of Study through a sound educational delivery system using best practices based on the content of a course and the maturity of the student, such as: tutorials, workshops, class-based instruction, study groups, self-study and independent readings. All students shall have dialog and support through a mentoring and coaching strategy. The emphasis is on "facts-based learning" and "using" the acquired information to answer questions and solve problems related to daily leadership and Christian service in the marketplaces of life. The ultimate objective of the **A.I.M.** Course of Study is to both inform and develop moral leadership and unselfish service to others. Students are taught to "buy up" each and every opportunity to advance the cause of moral excellence and spiritual influence in their daily lives.

(4)

YESHIVA TORAH INSTITUTE

Climbing the ladder toward New Testament Judaism

Yeshiva Torah Institute offers affordable interdisciplinary study and degree programs to serve the community of Biblical Judaism with interactive residency,distance learning elements and Internet dialog/ support designed to facilitate learning through innovative methodology and faculty support. A UNIT may be established in your Faith-based facility.

Purpose of the Yeshiva

The purpose of the Yeshiva Torah Institute is to equip true spiritual leaders for the propagation of (Biblical) Judaism with a curriculum for broadminded, knowledgeable and critical-thinking scholars leading to Licentiate in Jewish Studies for congregational leaders or authorized Rabbinical Ordination. Provided an ordained rabbi has sufficient academic background, the certified ordination would include an honorary Doctorate in Hebrew Letters. Classical approaches to subjects are complemented with academic and innovative methodologies. The instructional methods include classroom instruction, Internet interface, and a guided practicum for Licentiates and a mentored internship for candidates for ordination. These components combine to create a program of study with class-based credit that teaches students both theoretical knowledge and the skills to transform theory into practice. The ultimate goal of the Institute is to put forth competent leaders and rabbis well versed in the Jewish Torah capable of making wise judgments.

The core curriculum is focused on conceptual issues integrating methodologies that address historical concerns such as strata, composition and textual variants. The curriculum is designed to create knowledgeable, empathic leaders, who are skilled in the science and art of decision-making and who use mature judgment in rendering decisions. All classes include the study of primary material and developmental readings in relevant sources to produce additive and variant material. Adequate completion of each course/subject requires an essay submitted via the Internet.

QUANTIFIABLE ORTHODOXY AND ORTHOPRAXIS EXPERIENCED

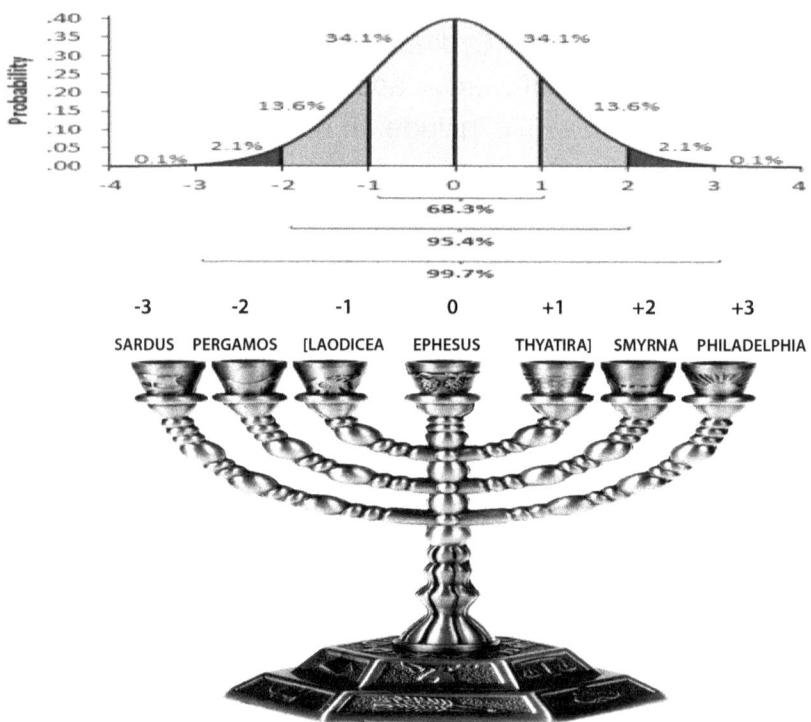

Comparison of the menorah with a sample of the seven congregations

(See Chapter Ten)

(5)

The class structure, textbooks, and curriculum of the Learning Centre are compatible with A.I.M. or C.A.F.E., and any other program that uses The EVERGREEN Devotional New Testament.

Faith-based subjects are presented in Workshops, Seminars, and Specialized Classes for Serious Learners, PLUS Academic Performance Training (academic guidance for High School and College Students). Full data from [www.globaledadvance.org] or greenoxon@aol.com

An Academic Performance Tutorial **A.P.T.** with students having particular trouble with a specific subject. **A.P.T.** posts dates/times/locations and subjects that are scheduled for high school and college students needing assistance.

Operational Delivery System for Faith-Based Education

Normally, religious or faith-based educational efforts are exempt from direct governmental supervision. Notwithstanding, an educational effort delivered by a faith-based entity should provide equal assurance that the facility, curriculum, faculty, and delivery system complies with academic, ethical and operational benchmarks. For example, in a private primary or secondary school using the (K-12) curriculum, students must pass state-sponsored tests to transfer to public or post-secondary schools. Also, denominations have "in house" training programs to certify or authorize individuals at various levels of service within the sectarian group; such as, deacon, lay minister, approved missionary, licensed pastor, or ordination; such credentialing is without state approval. Yet, when a religious or faith-based group forms a college or seminary that offers degrees with academic nomenclature, they are under direct supervision by the government.

With this in mind Global Educational Advance, Inc. is structuring an educational paradigm shift to assist faith-based groups with innovative educational solutions to meet the religious needs that a totally secular system neglects. This system includes providing religious groups with a faith-based **LEARNING CENTRE** that consists of a comprehensive **ACADEMY** with phased in options for a full-scale K-12 primary and/or secondary school or an enhanced "home schooling concept" that uses the **ACADEMY** as a resource for broader faculty and student socialization. The **ACADEMY** may be structured as a Student Advanced Tutoring **(S.A.T.)** Enterprise to prepare public or home-based students to pass standard or required exams. Also, the **ACADEMY** may be offered as an Information Technology (IT) based delivery system via Skype, interactive media similar to missionary or remote population guidance via shortwave radio or limited closed circuit-video where a home-based student or a small group may join a tutor for guidance, enrichment, or a full class session or homebased students may attend special tutoring or socialization sessions with other home-schooled students.

Those entities who choose not to institute a full public Academy may concentrate on the options of support tutoring for public and homebased students who need additional homework guidance or tutoring to pass required standardized grade-level tests or to reach an advanced level of achievement and be prepared for the normal S.A.T. TEST for college entry. Some academies may include:

- **D.A.S.H.** (Directed Academic Study Helpline) to assist students via telephone or facetime calls.
- **H.O.S.T.** (Homeschool Official Site for Tutorials and Testing);
- **P.U.S.H.** (Public Unit Student Assistance) where students in need may receive additional tutoring, coaching, or encouragement to achieve.
- Advance Performance Training **(A.P.T.)** may be used as part of the **S.A.T.** Enterprise to prepare students for state standardized tests, or **SAT TEST** for college entrance.

The LEARNING CENTRE includes an Alpha Institute of Ministry (**A.I.M.**) with a **C.A.F.E.** curriculum for Community and Family Education that replaces youth and adult church-related Bible study and leadership training with a 4-year plan to teach Bible content and practical courses with approved textbooks and syllabi to equip believers for lifestyle community service and practical ministry. The program of **A.I.M./C.A.F.E.** may also be used to train leadership for the local church or lay ministers to serve newly formed congregations as part of a church-planting or circuit structure of small groups.

Yeshiva Torah Institute is designed as outreach to teach converted Jews the relevant aspects of New Testament Judaism, the Christian lifestyle and both personal and group worship. A full curriculum is available for the **Yeshiva.**

The **LEARNING CENTRE** is the umbrella group, the **ACADEMY** is the K-12 operation with alternative delivery methods, **Alpha Institute of Ministry (A.I.M.)** is the post-secondary construct and Community and Family Education (**C.A.F.E**) is the faith-based curriculum for both faith-based instruction in the normal church education setting and a plan for outreach to the family and community. The options within the **LEARNING CENTRE** provide opportunities of faith-based groups of all sizes to participate in a comprehensive study and educational structure with creditable guidance and planned supervision.

Being a member unit (chartered, affiliated, or authorized) of a global system brings authenticity to the local endeavor provides interaction and fellowship with like-minded faith-based educators. This process brings a constructive paradigm shift in disciple-making, lifestyle mentoring, and leadership training for community service and missional living. The adoption of the thinking, behaviors, and practices of a missionary will engage others with the gospel and begin to fulfill the *Believer's Commission: "19. As you personally go, (going) therefore, and make disciples of all nations, baptizing them in the name of the Father, and of the Son, and of the Holy Spirit: 20. teaching them to observe all things whatever I have commanded you: and behold, I am with you always, even unto the end of the world. Amen." Matthew 28:19, 20 (EDNT).*

CHARTERING AFFILIATED AND AUTHORIZED ENTITIES

The Global AIM Network is designed to present missionaries and global faith-based entities an opportunity to structure a Learning Centre with an Academy (K-12) unit and an educational process that leads to advanced learning through **C.A.F.E.** (Community And Family Education) and **A.I.M.** (Alpha Institute of Ministry) to produce family life education, lifestyle guidance, community leadership and practical faith-based service. This opportunity includes both sacred text scriptural content and practical textbook study written especially for the purpose of advancing faith-based education with individuals and groups outside the normal academic environment. The parent organization, Global Education Advance, Inc., provides structure, guidance, and supervision to assist in both chartering and operating a quality local **LEARNING CENTRE** through a Network of like-minded individuals.

The Global AIM Network [www.globalaim.net] is not designed to qualify individuals for certification or credentials to function outside the realm of practical community and faith-based service. Rather the purpose is to equip faith-based individuals to become moral leaders in local places of worship and become moral citizens to provide practical mentoring and coaching to meet the needs of individuals and families in the community where they live and work.

The Network operates independently from government regulations, * but provides equal assurance that a Member entity has complied with a set of academic, ethical and operational benchmarks. The emphasis is on adequate facilities, quality leadership, consistent courses, and practical outcomes in a faith-based environment. Opportunities for professional interaction with individuals involved in similar faith-based efforts are provided by the Network in order to collaborate and develop fair, meaningful and functioning benchmarks for quality faith-based education in areas with limited educational opportunities. * Church and faith-based local educational efforts are normally exempt from government supervision.

The **Global AIM Network** has as a primary objective to charter, recognize, and encourage quality faith-based educational efforts in the local environment and structure an educational process for continuing practical and quality education where such is not normally available. The Network of local Learning Centers uses approved textbooks and receives guidance from Global Educational Advance, Inc., a nonprofit corporation in Tennessee working to bring transformative and constructive change to communities through various programming for development and continued support for practical education to benefit the young, the disadvantaged, and those who feel a call to missional lifestyle beyond their local community and into global opportunities. The Network is based in Tennessee but operates with a global vision assisting community-based groups, NGO's, prison study groups, faith-based educational efforts, and tertiary/post-secondary education with programs, projects, and services: developing curriculum, textbooks, library and learning resources, and funding. Presently the Network offers community groups creative programs that produce constructive change in individuals, positive change in family life, spiritual progress in faith-based groups, and positive social change in communities touched by faith-based ministry.

The leaders of Global Educational Advance, Inc. and Global AIM Network are experienced educators with credentials and professorial experience in education as well as local, regional, and global educational, ministry, and missional involvement. Their skills and knowledge in many aspects of secondary and post-secondary education, continuing education, and faith-based education and ministry are made available to participants in the Network. Additional details may be found on these Internet sites: www.globaledadvance.org, www.gea-books.com and www.globalaim.net [global sites are being updated to include data in this document.] or by correspondence to Global Educational Advance, Inc., 345 Barton Road, Suite 11, Dayton, TN 37321-7635 or greenoxon2@gmail.com.

Three Levels of Membership

1. There are three levels of Network Membership and Affiliation Official Chartering for **Probationary Membership** in the After six-months to one (1) year of Probationary Membership, an entity may apply for the **Affiliation** level and ask to be observed and evaluated for meeting minimum benchmark standards for a specific three (3) year endorsement in the chosen aspects of the LEARNING CENTRE programs.

2. An entity with Affiliation, may apply for full **Authorization** after an adequate Self-Evaluation

Report that includes data on an adequate operation for three (3) years. The Network will arrange an official site visit. With a positive Site Visit Report, an entity may be granted Authorization for five (5) years.

3. Continued Authorization requires adequate annual reports for five (5) years with continued observation and evaluation throughout the Re-authorizing Process Network.

4. Entities that fail to meet Network Operational Benchmarks, after adequate warning, may be dropped from Membership or be lowered in status to the level of compliance.

5. Entities dropped from Membership may re-apply after six-months to one (1) year of adequate operation.

6. Adequate operation includes: acceptable facilities, adequate faculty, approved curr6iculum, satisfactory records, and available student outcome data.

Chartering and Authorization is normally a voluntary process that educational entities assume to affirm they meet basic social, educational benchmarks, behave ethically, and employ appropriate quality assurance efforts. The process includes documentation and confirmation of adequate facilities, qualified faculty, competent leadership, and expected student outcomes. The original Charter and Membership is issued after evaluation of a completed application adequately reviewed by the Network Authorizing Group. Charter and Membership indicates that the educational entity has experienced a detailed peer review. Affiliation means approval of the operation, faculty, curriculum and quality assurance plans. Authorization implies adequate operation, ongoing development, adherence to established benchmarks, adequate student outcomes, and demonstrated advocacy for a stated mission. Note the steps following initial Membership:

1. The process is continued by annual reporting, inspection visits that include an official examination and verification of student records, institutional documents of teachers, curriculum, and appropriate facilities with scheduled use.

2. A self-evaluation, identifying strengths and weaknesses of the educational process, is both significant and ongoing. The process compares operations and curriculum to established benchmarks and recognizes needed improvements.

3. The self-evaluation process is verified by off-site evaluators who discuss appropriate matters with relevant constituencies.

4. The Network Authorizing Group regularly reviews materials from each Chartered, Affiliated and Authorized entity in accordance with the available educational information to provide a continued level of Membership in the Network.

5. The Network periodically releases via Internet the status of entities based on a Descriptive Report related to the self-evaluation and compliance with identified benchmark standards.

6. Chartered, Affiliated, or Authorized entities may respond to the Descriptive Report and submit

additional data to demonstrate further compliance with benchmark standards.

7. Chartered or Affiliated entities may use curriculum, textbooks, and receive minimum guidance from Global Educational Advance, Inc., but the Authorizing Process and the Re-Authorizing reviews are the basis for Membership and the Network's ability to ensure the quality of the operation and learning process offered by Membership entities within the context of their stated mission.

7

AUGMENT Outreach By A Nonsectarian Worldview And Extend Evangelism Through Missionary Support

– a value added asset to enable believers to participate in global outreach through personal and financial support.

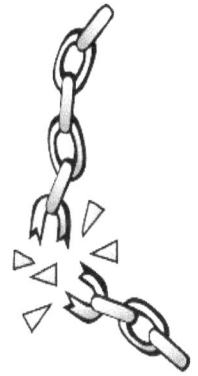

Weak links are a liability to missionary outreach. The chain of missionary evangelism is stronger than the weak links caused by limited knowledge of the results of conversion which leads to lifestyle changes. Those weak links did not experience *"old things have passed away; all things have become new.* "Believers who walk in fellowship with the Lord, normally develop a missional lifestyle and are committed to an outreach witness and evangelism to grow the kingdom.

When a link breaks the chain is made shorter; it may reach to Jerusalem, Judea, and Samaria, but may not be long enough to reach the farthest part of the earth.

The Challenge of Jesus and the reason Jesus asked the Father to send the Holy Spirit was to bring the disciples miraculous ability and strength to follow the instructions and stay on course for the distance. If the world is to be reached with the lessons of grace, the message must be protected by strengthening the weak links in the chain of evangelism.

The Missionary challenge was to reach the uttermost part of the earth, not to pick and choose the close or the easiest places. The challenge of Jesus to his close followers was *"as you go into all the world make disciples and became a mandate for all born again believes walking in fellowship with the Lord..* To make disciples, converts must be identified with the Trinity through baptism, and taught all that Jesus began to do and teach from the beginning of His ministry until the Ascension. (Acts 1:1ff) This is why local Faith-based groups must accept this challenge, have a nonsectarian worldview and strengthen the weak links in the chain of missionary outreach. This is true missionary support. Missions needs people and time as well as money.

Believers must practice the presence of Jesus. He promised to be with us on the journey to the farthest parts of the earth by His statement *"I am with you always to the end of the world."* He is with us Now, He "always" will be with us, even to the end of the journey. This promise makes the journey a prosperous one. The end of the journey is worth the hardships! These words of Paul are a comfort to those who journey on the road less traveled.

> *16. the Holy Spirit joins with our human spirit confirming that we are the children of God: 17. since we are children, then heirs, and fellow-heirs with Christ; if we suffer together we may also be glorified together. 18.* **For I consider the sufferings we now endure not worthy**

to be compared with the glory about to be revealed in us. 19. All creation is yearning expecting to see the appearance of the children of God. (Romans 8:16-19 EDNT)

Avoid Name Brand Religion and Freeze Frame Thinking

A cultural framework for doctrine has created a brand name concept for American Christianity. This development was based on the writings of past theologians and produced a freeze frame thinking not relevant to the present generation. Believers have failed to transmit adequate experiential knowledge of the Christian life to succeeding generations to make genuine converts. This, coupled with the mobility of society, has produced complex and confusing relationships within American congregations. Consequently, preachers and parents unintentionally hinder the conversion of the next generation to the Christian Faith. To make Christianity viable in the Twenty-first Century, there must be an internal redirection of the soul.

God is not dead! Religion did not fade away as an old soldier. The predictions concerning the early demise of religion were premature. Friedrich Nietzsche's 1882 calculation about the early decline in religious faith was wrong. Both Bernard Shaw and H. G. Wells predicted an end to what they called the "religious phase" of history; they were wrong. Even as late as mid-century, Julian Huxley wrote about "God's last fading smile" and compared it to the grin of a Cheshire cat. None of these secular prophets were correct. Although attendance at religious meetings has declined, a basic belief in God remains deep in the human psychic. What is lacking is the dynamic faith that makes life a shared journey with God. Missing is a genuine togetherness and moral agreement in the faith-based community. What is needed is a non-sectarian view of the world and the Word of God. Faith-based operations must get back to One Lord, One Faith, One Baptism and One Common Objective: to reach the world with redemptive grace.

A Common Agenda

One faith-based group or one religion will never produce world peace or feed the children or care for the sick and dying. One group cannot eliminate poverty, violence, drugs, human trafficking or complete global moral change. There must be a common agenda to make people moral citizens of the world before they can become mystical citizens of heaven. Synergetic cooperation is not to suggest a least common denominator religion or that Judaism, Islam or Christianity should lose their culture or compromise their sacred reality. Culture and tradition are social glue that holds religions together. This cultural bonding is strong, but compromise (*a "together-promise" agreement*) is a necessary part of the way forward that leaves no one behind. Where organized groups choose not to function, personal action can make a difference and break down some of the barriers to an action agenda that could strengthen the One Lord-One Faith message. Perhaps, a better missionary "second front" in the global spiritual battle or a fresh and strategic "guerilla warfare" effort could make a difference. Remember, the goal for a global outreach is not domination or control, but emancipation from poverty and violence and liberty to choose a personal and eternal destiny in the hands of Providence.

For this to happen, the barriers to personal faith and action must be removed.

Second Front and Guerilla Warfare

A generic least common denominator religion is not the answer, there must a re-energized approach to faith-based operations on three fronts: fervent local worship groups, eager "second front" outreach units which initiate teaching/learning centers, and strategic "guerilla warfare" activity behind the lines to teach the teachable and reach the reachable. No one religion has been able to reach all the population of any one location. In fact, all the major monotheistic religions have divisions that limit their global effectiveness. Each group behaving as if they have found the "Holy Grail" and have exclusive access to the "secrets" of eternal redemption.

Little Common Ground

Tragically, there is little common ground; however, moral leadership must start somewhere and seek to make a difference in the world. Provided the hostility and rivalry can be adjusted, gates in the dividing walls opened, and a common cause becomes self-evident, there is hope for a moral and faith-based agenda that can change the world one person at a time. This common ground must be faith-based and known to be true without ecclesiastical validation. The personal expression of faith is essential to this process.

Engle's Scale Reversed and Modified

Engle's Scale has been reversed and modified for this work to enable the reader to more clearly see the process of moving potential converts up the scale of understanding. Since many in the known world hold personal religious beliefs other than those of the monotheistic faiths, and have little awareness of a Supreme Being or no effective knowledge of faith-based operations, it is necessary to reach them where they are and move them up the scale until they develop a positive attitude and recognize the problem of being lost. As faith-based believers reach into the marketplace and the pools for potential converts, a clear contextual analysis is required before intervention strategies can be implemented.

Individuals and groups around the world are at different levels of non-awareness and awareness. One must recognize a declining scale to know at which point the person is open to the Gospel. For this work Engel's Scale has been reversed as an intervention strategies which may be imposed at different levels as individuals and groups move toward acceptance of Christianity. There is also a 1-7 positive scale for discipleship.

_____AWARENESS
- Awareness of Supreme Being —10l

No Effective Knowledge of Christianity —9 |

_____UNCONVERTED POOL
- Initial Awareness of Need —8 |
- Interest—Acceptance of Medium —7

_____ PERSONAL AWARENESS
- Awareness of Gospel —6
- Grasp of Implications —5

_____REALIZATION OF NEED
- Positive Attitude--4
- Personal Problem Recognition—3

_____ DECISION TO ACT
- Challenge/Decision to Act—2

_____ ENCOUNTER
- Repentance/Faith in Christ--1

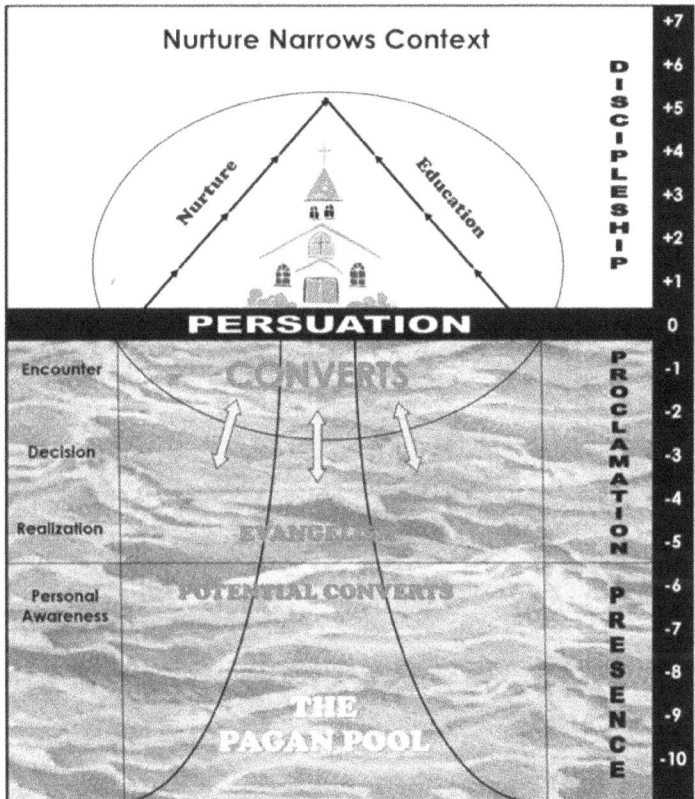

Figure - Modified Engel's Scale --a modified Engel's scale must be understood to assure communication with the pagan pools

Study the Modified Engel's Scale above to better understand the necessary steps to bring the message of saving grace to the lost. Please notice the process that brings individuals to a Decision to Act and Repentance at minus 2 and 1. When this is attempted earlier, it usually fails.

Periods of awareness and intervention by Christians are required prior to a direct encounter that may or may not lead to lead to a conversion experience.. The periods are:

1. Awareness (10-6)
2. Realization (5)
3. A Period of Decision (4-2)
4. Encounter (1)

Intervention strategies take three forms:

a) A Ministry of Presence (10-6)

b) A Period of Proclamation (5-2)

c) A Time of Persuasion (1)

Once an Encounter is made during the time of persuasion, the individuals involved must make a firm decision. This decision begins a Period of Incorporation. Converts must be nourished and nurtured through Discipleship Training into the active life of a Christian. Several steps are evident:

1. Post-decision Evaluation
2. Incorporation
3. Personal Fruitfulness
4. Conceptual Growth
5. Discovery of Spiritual Gifts
6. Incarnational (Social) Growth
7. Stewardship
8. Prayer
9. Use of Spiritual Gifts

10. Witness – Reproduction

The Period of Incorporation requires the Christian community to assist the convert in learning to follow Christ. These steps are:

a) Discipleship

b) Christian Education

c) Body Life

d) Koinonia (fellowship)

e) Diakonia (service)

> Personal viewpoints and values are major factors that impact the daily struggle of leaders and managers. This is true in all aspects of life, but especially true at the place of work. Most organized enterprises today talk about good business to guide the required effort to achieve a profitable status. However, saying the right words is the easy part; doing the work to make the words happen is the struggle. This is where faith-based principles and values influence the decision and behavior process in organizations.

MISSIONAL LIFESTYLE (Infinity #)
Active Witnessing

An exponential Explosion in Evangelism

During World War II in a Luftwaffe Prison Camp in England that consisted only of German airmen, a modern exponential explosion of conversion occurred. From the testimony of a Medical Doctor present, a group of British women decided an act of Christian charity would be to share their bread ration with the German airmen. When half-loafs of bread were placed on the table, the German ranking officer complained to Dr. A. E. Wilder-Smith about the half rations. When he was told about the women sharing their bread ration, it opened his heart to Dr. Wilder-Smith's witness of God's Saving Grace. It is a record of exponential conversion where most of the German inmates of the prisoner of war camp embraced Christian conversion. It is believed that Christian acts of kindness in lifestyle witness can enlarge the kingdom. Perhaps the assembly celebration should produce a daily lifestyle witness that could be expressed as the sweet bread of life sacrificially shared. Shared bread was like CAKE –Christian Acts of Kindness Each-day.

Rediscovering the Missional Identity

The *missional* construct rediscovers the true identity of *"those belonging to the Lord"* as spiritual witnesses to the world and understands the final words of Jesus to His followers, as a Lifestyle Challenge to Believers rather than a program for an organized house of worship. In the scripture below please notice that Jesus was speaking directly to His followers about **His authority and power** and **sharing what He expected in their future lifestyle,** *"as you go make disciples of all nations"* reminding **them to identify future disciples with the work of the Godhead**: the Father is the Forgiver; the Son is the Savior; the Holy Spirit is the Comforter, Enlightener, and *Paraclete* (called to assist and encourage) enabling believers to live a missional lifestyle and realize that the end is worth the spiritual journey.

Moving Beyond Structured Programs

The construct of missional in this book moves beyond the programs of structured denominations, organized local assemblies, and Faith-based Christian gatherings. Missional does not see the gathering "places" for worship as primarily an organized activity, but rather the individual's response to the worth-ship of God in the act of personal worship. A missional reality goes beyond the pursuit of churchgoing and the reaching of converts to the process of individual involvement in "disciple making" and funding the global Kingdom advance.

A "value-added" Asset

Salvation and growth in grace and knowledge are a "value added" asset to enable believers to participate in a global outreach and understand how Kingdom Economics and Personal Wealth contribute to the stability of the family and the support and operation of personalized ministries. A missional mindset should produce in believers the attributes and attitudes that demonstrate their ability and predisposition in a lifestyle that is recognized by the community. Witnessing is literally "lifestyle behavior" in contrast to that of non-believers and is the tried and true method of advancing the Kingdom of God.

Academic and Cultural Bias

In the England of 1604-1611, the concept of building an Empire was just beginning. To build a British Empire required Englishmen to leave their island fortress and colonize the new world. The Court of Queen Elizabeth and the golden age of English art, literature, and adventure were precursors to this effort. It was 1585 when the first effort to export the golden age was made "to go across the sea" and settle the new land "Virginia," named after the virgin Queen. Although this group nearly starved before Sir Frances Drake rescued the survivors, the concept of "go and do" was firmly established in the minds of English achievers. Consequently, the translators seeking to please the new king, James, used an obscure Greek rule to translate a participle into an imperative: "*Go into all the world…*" This created a program of pressure that caused an artificial incentive that negates the power of personal experience -- which is the true means of advancing Christianity. The Challenge of Jesus supports a missional lifestyle of making disciples *"as you go"* rather than a program of *"go and do."* The verses below make clear the intention of Jesus:

> *14. Afterward He appeared to the eleven as they were eating, and reproved for their lack of faith and stubbornness, because they did not believe those who had seen Him after He stood up from the grave. 15. And He said,* **As you journey to the whole world, proclaim a good message to every inhabitant. 16. He who believes and is baptized will be saved;** *but he who believes not will be condemned. (Mark 16:14-18 EDNT)*

> *45. Then He opened their understanding, that they might grasp the meaning of the scriptures. 46. And said, Scripture clearly says that Messiah should suffer, and stand up from the grave the third day: 47. and* **that repentance and forgiveness of sins should be proclaimed in His name among all nations, starting at Jerusalem. 48. And you are witnesses of**

these things. 49. And, behold, I send the promise of My Father: but you must wait expectantly in the city of Jerusalem, until you be clothed with ability and heavenly strength. (Luke 24:45-49 EDNT)

19. Then the same day at evening, being the day one of the week, when the doors were shut where the disciples were assembled for fear of the Jews, Jesus came and stood among them, and said, Peace to you. 20. And when He had spoken, He showed them His hands and side. When the disciples saw the Lord, they were glad. 21. **Then Jesus said again, Peace to you: <u>as my Father, has sent Me, even so send I you.</u> 22. And when He said this, He breathed on them, and said, Receive the Holy Spiri**t: *(John 20:19-22 EDNT)*

6. On one occasion the apostles asked Him, Lord will you now restore the kingdom to Israel? 7. He answered, It is not for you to know the period of time or the specific season, that is only in the Father's authority. 8. **But you shall receive miraculous ability and strength, after the Holy Spirit is come upon you: and you shall be My witnesses unto the death both in Jerusalem, and in all Judaea, and in Samaria, and continually into the farthest part of the earth.** *(Acts 1:6-8 EDNT)*

A Form of Godliness

Gathering in a particular place to be entertained or participate in a form of worship that fails to demonstrate the value of God in all aspects of life is a fraud. A form of godliness in worship without power or lifestyle behavior that is not missional does not acknowledge the *"worth-ship"* of God or prompt the taking of the message of peace, love, and eternal life to the world. It is less than pure religion. Faith-based worship should impact a missional reality in the life of Believers and encourage a positive worldview. The words of James, the forceful leader of a pristine congregation of early believers in Jerusalem are appropriate here:

A Message to Early Believers

9. Wherefore, my cherished band of believers let everyone be swift to hear, slow to speak, slow to wrath: 19. because of the righteousness of God, let everyone be ready listeners, slow to express our mind, slow to take offence: 20. for anger does not bear fruit acceptable to God. 21. **Wherefore put aside all moral corruption and the abundance of worthless behavior and receive with a teachable spirit the firmly established word, which is able to make safe that spiritual part of you that determines all behavior.**

A Muddled Message

Western world leadership muddled the message of grace by accepting a watered-down orthodoxy which included variations of sectarian dogma, geographical culture, personal convictions, and social attitudes that predetermine how situations will be viewed, questions answered, and sacred scripture construed. It appears they understand the Gospel and the benefits of religion "*as a commodity*" available only for habitual church-goers. Such self-righteous groups are better described as having *"name brand religion"* which uses history and events as *"freeze-frame theology"* to defend their lack of relevance to the lives of real people and humanity. This includes the matter of faith-based economics and personal wealth.

> *1. Know this that dangerous times will come in the last days. 2. For men will be self-lovers,* **lovers of money**, *arrogant boasters, treating God and sacred things disrespectfully, disobedient to parents, unthankful, wicked, 3. without family affection, true-breakers, false accusers, without sexual restraint, violent, despisers of all that is good, 4. traitors, stubborn, lovers of pleasure more than lovers of God; 5.* **having an outward façade of religion, but rejecting the moral instructions and are strangers to the influence of the Spirit:** *from such turn away. (2 Timothy 3:1-5 EDNT*

An Unlearned Lesson of History

The world did not learn the lesson the came from the fall of Germany. Germanic leadership was obvious in academics, business, inventions, and in the production of theological textbooks. Yet, their churches failed to influence the behavior of the population. This tragedy is clear in the life and death of Dietrich Bonhoeffer. During the buildup to WWII, Hitler and the Third Reich demonstrated their opposition to Judaism, began to control all religions and bring the German church under Nazi supervision. Bonhoeffer faced death in a Nazi prison because of his personal courage by resisting governmental control of the German church.

Concept of Principled Responsibility

Through the Confessing Church, Bonhoeffer began to develop his concepts of principled responsibility in relation to the spiritual life and resisted this infringement. During his imprisonment, he worked further on a lifestyle approach to discipleship. It took real courage to live the disciplined life during the Nazi period, but perhaps it takes more audacity and spiritual courage to resist secularization of the faith-based community in times of peace. Silently, civil government has encroached on the sacredness of marriage, life of the unborn, issues of death and dying, and some matters of conscience that have been the purview of the religion for centuries. Only missional behavior and lifestyle can resist this encroachment.

An Antecedent Obligation

Although Bonhoeffer made fragmentary suggestions about a time when there could be a "religion-less society," his insights and understanding developed during the cauldron and instability of war should alarm all faith-based people. These statements concerned the reality of Christian faith, not the formal, public expression of religion. He believed that faith-based people had an antecedent obligation that binds them together as a social force to certain responsibility. He suggested that the meanness of war annihilated this viable historical possibility for Germany and much of the world.

Faith and the Inhumanity of Conflict

Looking at the tragedy of armed conflict, Bonhoeffer understood that German preaching and teaching did not create a human conscience to prevent the inhumanity of armed conflict during the decades of two world wars. The tragedy of warfare crushed the internal principles by which Germany engaged the world and the wartime atrocities were committed by men who had been under the influence of the German church for decades. The tragedy, according to Bonhoeffer, was that the church seemed to have no influence on the social policies of the government or the behavior of the German soldier.

False Witness

To disguise religious activity as spiritual work is deception, sacrilege and a *"false witness"* in a list of things which God hates. (Proverbs 6:16-19) Camouflage is used as concealment when an adversary does not wish to be recognizable. Some disguise declining local participation in terms of a migrating population or changing communities. The obscuring of decline deceives the public by self-serving explanations; such as, redecorating buildings, adding space, landscaping, putting up new signs, or adding other trappings of progress and unnecessary embellishments to attempt to display prosperity.

The Despised Few Excuse

Some small groups claim the membership has settled to a *"despised few"* because of their emphasis on quality rather than quantity. Despite the method of concealment or the change in appurtenances of property, the influence faith-based group once had on the community has weakened or become nonexistent. Sponsored events have taken on a civil or social identity rather than being seen as a religious experience. These self-serving explanations have camouflaged the trend toward decline. The benefit and power of faith-based groups is slipping away, and no one seems to care. False and insincere forms of worship have been present and recorded in both the Old and New Testament, God declares:

> *"These people come near to me with their mouth and honor me with their lips, but their hearts are far from me. Their worship of me is based on merely human rules they have been taught. (Isaiah 29:13) "These people honor me with their lips, but their hearts are far from me." (Matthew 15:8)*

Negative Participation

A decline in weekly participation in religious activities is apparent. The lack of converts, the vanishing financial resources, the public disclosure of clergy immorality, all contribute to public contempt for institutionalized religion. Not only is there growing negative participation, most faith-based groups have been unable to maintain even the existing proportion of an increasing population. Children of leaders, families of the faithful and even the poor who historically have gladly received the regular preaching of the good news, are no longer present or have turned a deaf ear to the message. Frequently the poor look to secular society and charity operations to provide for their wants.

Most efforts to increase funding for basic human needs or true missionary outreach have slowly faltered. The pattern is not the same in all faith-based groups or communities, but the tendency exists and is alarming, infectious, and lethal for conservative or Bible-based operations. It appears that secular and materialistic concepts and constructs have become dominate in the thinking of most churchgoers and the general public.

The Marketplace Challenge

Traveling opens many doors for the gospel. The real challenge for a faith-based lifestyle is in the marketplace, out where the people are on a daily basis. At a New York airport waiting in line for a delayed night flight, two gentlemen were in line talking around me. When they would not break line, their conversation was forced on me. Understanding their frustration, my Delta Flying Colonel card was used to take them to a more private place to wait. The Crown Room was almost deserted. Soft drinks were in the refrigerator and little fish crackers on the counter, so the munching began.

Renewal and Commitment

After a while, one asked, "Do you work for the airline?" A negative answer was not sufficient, the follow up question dealt with my occupation. They were told about my travels, writing and speaking. One asked, "What do you write?" Sharing with them about discipleship, evangelism and dying churches, one said, "My church is spiritually dead, and I am too!" With this the other one decided to leave. Alone, God worked His mysterious process of renewal and commitment.

Involvement vs. Attendance

A note on Delta stationary from the Crown Room arrived in the mail. It listed "Seven things God did for me today." Spiritual outreach is not dead; the cause of Christ is alive and well; it is just functioning better on an individual basis than it is at the institutional level. Why is this happening? Faith-based leaders and parents have failed to develop a faith-based culture that includes the practice of personal witness to God's saving grace. Local congregations must seek to enhance the quality of daily lifestyle involvement by individuals rather than the quantity of attendance at a scheduled service.

A Changing Perspective

The construct for a *missional lifestyle* is clearly described as a changing perspective the Disciples. Included in this challenge is a refocusing on the Words of Jesus to include the real life and spiritual needs of a lost world, rather than obsessing about the unlimited materialistic wants close to home.

> *17. And when they saw Jesus, some doubted. 18. And Jesus came and spoke, saying,* **All authority has been committed to Me in heaven and in earth.** *19. As you personally go,* **(going)** *therefore, and* **make disciples** *of all nations,* **baptizing** *them in the name of the Father, and of the Son, and of the Holy Spirit: 20.* **teaching** *them to observe all things whatever I have commanded you: and behold, I am with you always, even unto the end of the world. Amen. (Matthew 28:17-20 EDNT)*

8

GROW Constituency By Multiplying Congregations

— reaching local people to form new fellowship and interest groups that become new congregations.

Lessons from the Life of Joseph

Genesis began with the Creation of all things and ended with "a coffin in Egypt." Genesis also taught through the life of Joseph, the proper personal behavior within a cross-cultural situation. Regardless of the negative aspects of his life, Joseph stood by his principles, adapted to the situation, understood the culture, took advantage of opportunities, kept faith with family and his God, served the people of a strange land, and finally by faith claimed his place in the Promised Land. Joseph made the best of a bad situation and because of his commitment to honesty, morality, and fairness, his life benefited all of Egypt and his own family. In the end he was buried in a parcel of land purchased by his father. The end was worth the journey.

Growing in a Multicultural Environment

How did the early faith-based movement, known as The Way, survive and grow in a multicultural society? How did a faith rooted deeply in Judaism maintain reliability and consistency confronted with the cross-cultural issues of those following Jesus? What were the antecedent causes for growth during the first 100 years? Why and how did their Faith-based gatherings grow within the Greco-Roman culture. How were communications handled between Hebrew, Greek and Latin? It seems that Latin and Greek were both official languages of the Roman Empire (with Latin remaining the one for the upper class) and the Jewish people concentrated on Hebrew. Yet a few educated leaders, Paul being a good example, were well acquainted with the languages used in the First Century.

The ability to read, write, and speak multiple languages was a foundation for development. Knowing the essential elements of Judaism and structure of Greco-Roman culture were a major asset in the New Testament era. Greek philosophic knowledge and the infrastructure of Roman roads and water systems opened trade and personal interaction among people during the first century of Christian influence. To arrive at the antecedent "WHY" one must understand the "HOW" by engaging the interrogatives: when, what, who, where, how many, how long, etc. When the "how" is understood, the antecedent "why" the pristine movement of Christianity grew will be known.

Genesis and Galatians recorded the Blessing of Abraham's Seeds (Galatians 3:7-9). Acts records that God gave particular territory to individuals and groups. (Acts 17: 26). Some made a territorial commitment and claimed their community. (2 Corinthians 10:13-16) Present day Christians sometimes leap frog over their community and concentrate on foreign lands. In the first two chapters of Acts one finds at least seven reasons for early growth and development:

11. The people were **accountable to a divine Person**. "This same Jesus" would return and they would give an account of their work.
12. The people **accepted a divine program** (lifestyle witnessing in Jerusalem, Judea, Samaria, and to the ends of the earth).
13. The people were **assured through divine promises** (Promise of the Holy Spirit and Christ's Return)
14. The people **accepted divinely chosen personnel** (12 Apostles, 70, anointed and sent ones, etc.)
15. The people were **anointed with divine power** (Spiritually equipped for lifestyle evangelism and all were teaching appropriately in all situations.)
16. The people were **active in directed proclamation**. (All witnessing and preaching/teaching in Acts were to people outside a Faith-based assembly.)
17. The people **agreed in common faith based behavior and participated in daily prayer**. (All things common, one mind, one faith, one accord, one place). This was the plan and remains God's way.

Globalizing the Gospel

Launching Mission Stations as a precursor for establishing a new place of worship is a most effective way to move forward and globalizing the gospel. The word "missions" has been defined improperly as home and foreign activity of the church. Missions is not foreign or domestic; Christian missions is everywhere by everyone at all times. In fact, every believer is a missionary without a capital letter. In fact, in an answer to a letter to Elizbeth Elliot about the death of her brother, she reprimanded me for using a capital "M" on Missionary. She stated that all believers were "missionaries" as part of the spiritual Divine Nurturing Attribute (DNA) of a convert when God breathes a spark of new life and *"old things pass away, and all things become new."* Conversion provides a spiritual element that produces a desire to serve and advance kingdom issues. A true convert will have the seed of this spiritual DNA and it should grow into active behavior and practices that shares the gospel message with anyone and everyone who will listen. This is the essence of Christian missions and the energy for expansion and growth of the kingdom of God.

Outreach and Expansion

Reaching new converts and planting new places for scriptural study and worship in neighborhoods where there are limited faith-based witnesses should be a commitment by every believer. A small congregation of 100 could easily "tithe" ten members to initiate a new outreach center in another location. The same would be true of a 500-member church, that could easily "tithe" fifty and a 1,000-member, church could "tithe" 100 families to open a new marketplace center for the gospel. However, the false concept that "bigger is better" seems to prevail and kingdom advance suffers.

Example of Nature

Take a look at nature: God's plan for growth. A single grain of corn can be multiplied by the process of planting and caring for the new plant. God's Eden commandment *"Be fruitful and multiply and replenish the earth"* could easily be understood in terms of obligatory reproduction in kind: chickens reproduce chickens, monkeys produce monkeys, human couples procreate children; likewise, believers should produce other believers. Would it not logically follow that places of worship should duplicate and plant new churches to grow the kingdom? Planting seeds of the gospel and transplanting believers to build additional teaching/learning centers and outreach stations should be a natural part of the mission of existing congregations. Was it an inaccuracy that Christian converts were considered to be born again into a new way of life and enabled by the Holy Spirit to behave their faith daily in an effective missional lifestyle?

Blueprint for Constructing a local Congregation

The blueprint for constructing an effective local congregation would be to take a positive stand and strive to move forward in all the areas where the congregation now fails to measure up to the essential elements of the great challenge of Jesus *"as you go into all the world make disciples."* Until weak areas are discovered and strengthened, the normally expected advance at the congregational level and progress in planting new churches will not develop. One must correct the inferior aspects of the present operation before a superior outreach plan can be developed. Failures must be diagnosed and corrected before a plan of action can be executed to expand kingdom operations in new areas.

The progressive decline of faith-based operations is not inevitable? The character and social fabric of the global society is complicated, and believers must work to make faith-based living viable in a pluralistic and multicultural society. Many believers are alive and reaching their communities. This is not true of the whole faith-based movement. Religion seems to be stagnant, fragmented, and unable to present a unified message to the public. One Lord, One Faith, One Baptism has become 300 sectarian groups divided by legalistic leaders, competing agendas, and opposing methodologies. The only hope of breaking the stained-glass barrier is an internal redirection of the soul that renews the spirit of "living by faith" which requires a missional attitude and lifestyle. Note the last words of Jesus before His Ascension in Acts 1: 8.

> …. *you shall receive miraculous ability and strength, after the Holy Spirit is come upon you: and you shall be My witnesses unto the death both in Jerusalem, and in all Judaea, and in Samaria, and continually into the farthest part of the earth.*

Vitality of Community Involvement

Agenda Priorities

Many problems of faith-based groups are agenda driven. The difference between a goal and a dream is an agenda. If it is merely a dream, one cannot establish a specific agenda. If one is not clear on basic philosophy, general objectives, and specific goals, the agenda will not work. Basically, the faith-based movement has lost the power of the Sunday punch because the First Day of the week has become the psychological last day. Consequently, it no longer sets the priorities and pace of faith-based activities for the week.

This creates a spirit of coercion that causes leadership to spend most of their time attempting to challenge constituency involvement in lifestyle witnessing. The congregation, in turn, is busy with frivolous things that have little value for kingdom advance; the busyness is simply the exercise in futility of an unproductive life. Strong arm tactics create a corporate methodology designed for outreach which seems to negate the power of personal initiative and individual experience. Complicated methods and over programming limits the mobilization of the congregation because the constituency does not understand the philosophy undergirding the methods.

When such programs fail, the people are usually blamed. Thus, the congregation becomes imprisoned by previous patterns, without contemporary priorities, and this perpetuates ineffective programming. Perhaps the greatest difficulty to reaching outside the four walls is when the building complex is presented as a field in which to work rather than a force which empowers outreach. Consequently, most of congregational energy is used to keep organizations alive, clergy and the congregation are often unaware that the organism is dying and that the community is not being served or influenced by their message or lifestyle.

Why does this happen? Sectarian positions cause leaders to split theological hairs which overshadows cooperative outreach. There is a conscious effort to advance a "go" strategy, rather than an "as you go" lifestyle among constituencies. This is done to keep traditional machinery in motion and causes a downgrading of proclamation of the Word. Finally, the preoccupation with details of programs and a multiplicity of causes rather than a purpose-centered commitment creates a growing gap between the pulpit and the pews.

Personnel Problems

Personnel problems begin with the leadership and weakens believers as the living Body of Christ. Accordingly, this produces weak links that endanger the chain of evangelism. Perhaps the most serious consequence of the weak pulpit is the preaching of cheap grace and easy believe-ism. The free grace of God did not come without a cost: it cost Jesus His life and requires a process of conversion, discipleship and a growth into a lifestyle witness. Although God has the power to perform the miracle of conversion; this is not done without the aid of the Holy Spirit and the willingness of the convert. It is a beginning and not the end of the process of growing in grace and knowledge. It should be remembered that *"you believe in one God; that is good, but the evil spirits also believe, and shake in fright."* (James 2:19)

Easy believe-ism produces poor converts and causes the congregation to accept individuals who have an intellectual acceptance of truth but often possess little experiential knowledge of the process that leads to Christian discipleship. Thus, the congregation has difficulty leading such weak converts into an active lifestyle that informs the general public that they are true disciple of grace. When professing converts do not grow in grace and knowledge, it is impossible to produce believers who can be entrusted with the saving witness as "apostles of the streets."

> *17. Even so faith without praiseworthy deeds, is like an unburied corpse left alone. 18. Yes, a man may affirm that he has faith, and not have deeds; show me faith apart from deeds, and I will show you faith by means of my deeds. 19. You say you believe in one God; that is good. But the evil spirits also believe and shake in fright. 20. Oh, worthless one, can you not perceive with certainty, that faith without deeds is a corpse? (James 2:17-20 EDNT)*

Why is this a problem? The chain of evangelism is shortened by weak converts that break and fail to develop the capacity for *agape* love for the lost. True sacred knowledge is not automatically transferred from head to heart to hand. When the people do not understand the phases of growth and development in disciple making, they attempt a "no holds barred" policy in attendance building and become concerned with quantity instead of quality and spiritual growth suffers within the congregation. Such behavior causes the people to be content with mediocrity and they settle to be "God's despised few." Thus, the congregation willingly settles for less than the best and suffers from spiritual diseases which strangulates growth and progress. A global outreach view is lost, and both the community and the family are neglected. Many fail to attend services and many who do attend become God evaders and permit things that distract their attention from the Word and worship. Therefore, there is little right living and/or positive social change in the family, the pews, or the community.

Fellowship Problems

As the people concentrate on a narrow definition of fellowship, a "no harvest" philosophy grows. Many programs and activities have no outreach objective. Leaders push activities that keep people happy and stay busy within the walls of the building. This precipitates a "come" strategy where the church doors are opened, and they wait for people to come. This reminds me of General Booth and his Salvation Army. When his unorthodox methods were challenged, he responded, *"You ring a church bell which says, 'come to church… come to church'-- we use the Bass Drum which says, 'Fitch 'um.. fitch 'um and we get um!'"*

Since fellowship alone is not strong enough to hold any group together, an active constituency drift exists that is often concealed by programs and camouflaged scheduled activities. In an effort to seek and maintain connection with a sectarian group, local congregations adjust their program and activities to maintain a linkage with a parent group rather than building a kingdom connection with the community. This produces a paternalism that often prevents community problem solving and causes an over dependency on external sectarian guidance. The fellowship activities also wall in the people and isolate them from potential converts in the community.

> *Genesis 1:11 taught that the "seed was within the fruit." Jesus shared in John 15:16 -17 "You have not chosen me, but I have chosen you,*

and appointed you to go out and bring in fruit, and that your fruit should remain: and that you should obtain answers to your prayers to make them fruitful. 17. These things I command you, so that you may love one another." The search for fellowship and entertainment in church programming also causes the constituency to place priority on secondary projects and may be responsible for individuals being caught in the hustle of activities which leave no time for family life or sharing the message of grace.

Renewal Problems

Somehow in the whole scheme of renewal, the dynamic structure of the church is disregarded, and the automatic nature of revival is frustrated. A basic problem is the neglect of the priesthood of believer's that causes a "passive sheep" structure to prevail within the congregation and generally leads to the church taking a wrong route to renewal. The courage to prune personnel and programs and to administer the cure for spiritual disease is almost nonexistent. Both clergy and laity seem to be preoccupied with program, personnel, organization or fellowship at the expense of renewal. Consequently, men unintentionally hinder the process of renewal in the life of the congregation.

> To make Christianity viable in the
> Twenty-first Century, there must
> be an internal redirection of the soul
> which includes morality, ethics, and a
> nonsectarian approach to a evangelism
> and disciple making.

9

ADVANCE The Kingdom By Planting Churches

— establishing teaching/learning centers and mission stations that develop into places of worship.

Foundational Stones for a New Congregation
Based on Paul's Message to the Thessalonians

The scriptural foundation stones for this work were found in Paul's first letters to a new congregation. Paul wrote to the Thessalonians from Corinth around AD 50-51. The congregation was established the year before during a short stay of a missionary team. The Jews of Thessalonica rejected Paul's ministry during three Sabbaths in the synagogue; consequently, the team moved to the city and the people heard the good news gladly. A pristine congregation was established that was unspoiled, a gathering of believers who *belonged to the Lord.* While on his way to Corinth, Paul sent Timothy back to check on the condition of the new believers.

When Timothy's report came that the converts were doing well but had some misconceptions regarding the Second Coming of Christ, Paul was concerned. The connection of Paul and his ministry team with the Thessalonians was deep and abiding. Timothy's report was a check on the quality of their relationship, fellowship, teaching, and worship. The foundation stones for this congregation were truly relational; they were solidly connected to God, each other, and the ministry team who brought them the gospel message.

Oldest Preserved Work of Paul

Thessalonians is possibly the oldest preserved written work of Paul. It is our judgment that Paul's writing of Thessalonians was one message in two parts. The content of both parts was parallel and based on Timothy's Report. Paul wrote to encourage believers to be steadfast in persecution and specifically described events preceding the *Parousia*. He illustrated the stability of the believer's life and encouraged converts to reject worldliness and live by moral principles. Paul dealt with their misunderstandings and reviewed both the relational conduct of the team and the content of the preaching/teaching during their short stay in Thessalonica. It appears that Paul believed a knowledge of the imminent return of Christ was essential to the spiritual foundation and function of the assembled believers and their missional lifestyle. This pristine work of Paul becomes a pattern for church planting, reaching converts, conversion follow-up, and discipleship making of young believers. Note the words of Jesus in the Gospel of John:

> *15. I no longer call you (servants) or bond-slaves; because a bond-slave does not know what his Lord does:* **but you I have called friends; for all things that I have heard of my Father I have made known to you.** *16. You have not chosen me, but I have chosen*

*you, and **appointed you to go out and bring in fruit, and that your fruit should remain:** and that <u>you should obtain answers to your prayers to make them fruitful.</u> 17. These things I command you, so that you may love one another. (John 15:15-17 EDNT)*

Scriptural Study to Support this Book
(THESSALONIANS)

A study of Thessalonians would provide the reader the foundation stones for planting a Faith-based congregation and a working model for growing a new congregation. A study outline of the message and the author's rendering of the *koine* Greek into a devotional language provides guidance. Planting a church is an individual process and requires the same steps as growing a garden.

Some older folk remember the hard times when families were urged to plant vegetable gardens to supplement their food supply. Growing a garden also taught families, especially the young, that God was involved in the process, but there was plenty of work for the Gardner. I am reminded of my Grandfather's award-winning crop of corn. One Sunday a city slicker visited his church and was invited to Sunday lunch. After the meal grandfather proudly took the visitor to see his award-winning crop. The visitor thought my grandfather was too proud of his work and *declared "You should give God credit for this crop. He provided the soil, the minerals, the rain and sunshine."* Grandfather's response was simply, *"God sure left a lot for me and the boys to do!"* Oh, a city slicker is someone who knows nothing about growing corn.

Gardens were so prevalent during the war years in Great Britain that everyone still calls their back yard a garden. Now in better times they grow flowers, ground cover and shrubbery. The young and the poor have forgotten what grandparents and parents knew about gardening. Planting and growing a garden not only teaches the young and the poor the value of growing fresh vegetables; it makes them aware of God's intervention in their lives. A garden must be touched by the Hand of God regardless of the hard work of cultivating the land. Guidance in growing a garden also provides knowledge that plants are different and that they need to be organized and given special care. This knowledge may assist the poor and the unemployed through hard times; also, learning the lost art of growing a garden may become a life-saver during hard times in the future. .

Planting and growing new mission stations, house churches, and teaching/learning centers that develop into new churches follows the same steps. Faith-based groups could use a vegetable garden as a practical and profitable teaching tool for the young. Paul, Silas, and Timothy worked together to plant a new church in Thessalonica. To our knowledge, their work is the best plan to clearly understand the human effort and the spiritual dimension of church planting. We have chosen to present this rendering of Paul's writings to the Thessalonians as a starting place for any would be church planter. Study it well and remember it is not only human effort, the work must be touched by the Hand of God. Yet, the human element and labor must not be neglected. Dr. Green had the privilege of planting several new churches in his early ministry.

A Personal Example

As a young minister, he would go to a town without many churches and search for a suitable place to start. Usually, he found an empty building that needed repairs and search for the owner. Asking if it were available for rent, he would usually say it needs lots of repairs, negotiating with the owner to do the repairs in exchange for free rent for six months and reasonable rent for the next six months, The repair work would begin.

Going to a local store and buying 2 or 3 gallons of paint and several paint brushes, he would start painting the front of the building. As men came by to ask what and why work was being done on the building, the response was *"it's a free job to get free rent to have a place for singing and praying. How about taking a paint brush and helping?"* Before the day was over, the front was painted, and they were ready to start inside. The extra workers would be thanked for their help and asked for more assistance to clean, scrub, paint and build a small stage, pulpit, and homemade benches. Going to a local lumber yard and asking for cull lumber to make benches for people to listen to music. Surprisingly, they would often point to a cull lumber pile and let us pick the scrap boards.

By the time the building was ready for the first service there were about 25 adult volunteers, both men and women, with sweat equity in the preparation of the building. They came and brought family and friends to the first service. Some would bring guitars or an accordion to assist with the singing. A short devotional homily was presented after the singing, and the planting of a faith-based congregation in a new place was beginning. After about 6 months, someone would be found to "pastor the flock," and a small crew would move to another place and with the assistance of God and others plant a new congregation. Fifty (50) years later several of these early local congregations were continuing to worship and disciple new converts for the kingdom. The teamwork that planted the church at Thessalonica was the guide in planting churches. It behooves anyone wishing to plant a new church or grow an existing congregation to study the messages Paul sent to the Thessalonians. Note the outline below:

A NEW TESTAMENT MODEL FOR CHURCH PLANTING

I. A RELATIONAL CONGREGATION MUST HAVE TOGETHERNESS [1:1-4]

How did they proceed?

A team effort 1. Paul, and Silas, and Timothy,

A togetherness in Christ *to the congregation assembled at Thessalonica, in union with God the Father and the Master Jesus Christ: favor to you and peace of heart, from God our Father, and the Lord Jesus Christ.*

A continued intercessory prayer *2. We always give thanks to God for you all, without ceasing making mention of you in our prayers;*

Activity inspired by faith *3. Remembering your faith that produced works, [subjective genitive]*

A love that prompts labor *and love that prompted labor,*

A hope that brings endurance *and hope in the Lord Jesus Christ that brought about endurance before God and our Father;*

An experiential knowledge that God loves each one *4. Knowing beloved brethren that you have been chosen of God.*

II. A RELATIONAL CONGREGATION REQUIRES PREACHING THAT PRODUCES EVIDENCE OF LIFESTYLE CHANGE
[1:5-10; Acts 11:26]

What did they share of the gospel?

How was the Gospel transmitted? *5. For our good news came not only in human speech, but also in words with innate power, and in the Holy Spirit,*

What was the substance of the Gospel? *and crammed full of conviction, as you know what kind of men we were among you for your sake.*

What were the changes in converts 1:6-10;

Converts must reproduce the soul-winner's faith? *6. And you became imitators of us, and of the Master, having accepted the word on a narrow path, but with joy of the Holy Spirit:*

What was the personal impact of the Gospel? *7. So, you became a model for all the believers in Macedonia and Achaia.*

Converts became witnesses. *8. For from you echoed out the word of the Master not only in Macedonia and Achaia, but also in every place your trust God-ward is overflowed abroad, so that we do not need to speak a word; 9. For others are telling of their own accord, what welcome you gave us,*

Changed! *and how your* ***turned*** *from idols*

Serving! *to* ***serve*** *the living and sincere God;*

Waiting! *10. And to confidently wait the return of God's Son from heaven, whom he raised from a corpse, even Jesus our rescuer from the coming wrath.*

III. RELATIONSHIPS BASED ON CONVERTS VIEW OF THE SOUL-WINNER (2:1-12)

First impression of the soul-winner. *2:1 For you know, brethren, that the good effect of our entering in unto you, continues:*

The full story of soul-winner's fluency of Speech 2:2-12 *2. But even after cruel and unfair treatment at Philippi, with Godly fluency in speech we brought you good news with much anxiety and conflict.*

Exhorting (facts) *3. Yet our appeal to you was not based on false or degraded thinking nor on cunning craftiness: 4. But passing God's scrutiny, He judged us fit to be entrusted with the good news: when we speak, it is not to please men, but God who examines our hearts. 5. You know that we never used the language of flattery, and God knows we never attempted to enrich ourselves: 6. For we never sought praise from you or others, when we might have been burdensome to you as apostles of Christ.*

Encouraging (decisions) *7. But we were tender among you, even* **as a nursing mother** *warmly takes pleasure in her children: 8. So affectionately longing for you, we were willing to share with you, not only the gospel of God, but also well pleased to share our lives, because you were valued by us. 9. You remember, brethren, our long and hard labor night and day, because we would not burden you for expenses, but freely preached the gospel of God unto you. 10. You are witnesses and so is God, how upright, honest and blameless was our conduct among you that believe:*

Educating Discipleship and discipline *11. As you know how we encouraged, comforted, and charged every one of you,* **as a father treats his children***, 12. that you would lead a life worthy of God, who has called you unto the glory of His kingdom.*

IV. THE WORD OF GOD AS TRANSFORMING TRUTH
(2:13-16)

Transformation came by a word of hearing (listening)

Transformation came by a word of revelation (eye-opener)

Transformation came by a word of faith (confidence, conviction) *13. This is why we give thanks to God without let* up, because the word of God you heard from us, you willingly welcomed not as the words of men, but as the true word of God which sets in operation an effectual work in you that believe.

There was opposition to the Word 14. For you became imitators of the brothers in God's assemblies in Judaea who gathered in Christ Jesus, for you also have suffered similar things of your own tribesmen, just as they have from the Jews: 15. The men who killed the Lord Jesus and their own prophets also persecuted us. They displeased God and showed themselves the enemies of mankind;

There will be reckoning for opposition to the Word (accounting) 16. Hindering us from speaking to the nations that they might (believe and) be saved, they keep filling up the measure of their sins, and now God's final vengeance has fallen on them.

How did Soul-winner show concern for converts when Satan placed obstacles to receiving the Word 2:17-3:13

Bereaved by absence 17. We brethren being orphaned from you for a short while in person, not in spirit, but desiring abundantly to see your face with great longing.

Hindered by Satan 18. I, Paul, planned a journey to you more than once, but Satan put obstacles in our way.

Praise for converts 19. For you alone are our hope, our joy, and crown of rejoicing in the presence of our Lord Jesus Christ at his coming. 20. All our pride and delight is in you.

Desire for converts stability/comfort 3:1-9 1. When we could no longer bear up under the strain of separation, it seemed good to be left in Athens alone; 2. I sent Timothy, our brother, fellow laborer in the gospel of Christ and minister of God, to establish you and comfort you concerning your faith: 3. There must be no wavering because of these trials: you know that this is our appointed lot. 4. When we visited you, we told you that we must suffer tribulations; now you see it has come to pass. 5. When I could no longer endure, I sent to know your faith, lest by some means the tempter had tempted you, and our labor was unproductive. 6. But now that Timothy has returned *from you and brought us good news of your faith and love, and that you always had good memory of us, desiring to see us as we also longed to see you. 7. Brethren your faith has brought us comfort in the midst of difficulties and trials. 8. For now life is worth living, if you stand fast in the Lord. 9. What thanks can we return to God for you and all the rejoicing we have because of you before God;*

Provision for Believers lack *10. night and day, we keep on praying that we might see your face and complete all that is lacking in your faith?*

Perfection of faith (learning to believe and trust)
11. Now may God Himself and our Father, and the Lord Jesus Christ, direct our journey to you. 12. And may the Lord increase you and cause you to abound in love one toward another, and toward all men, even as we do toward you:

Strengthen your hearts and establish in holiness *13. in order that He may strengthen your hearts, so you may be blameless in holiness before God, who is our Father at the coming of our Lord Jesus with all His saints.*

V. BELIEVERS IN A RELATIONAL CONGREGATION WILL ABOUND IN ABSTINENCE How? (4:1-8)

Believers separated from heathen immorality *1. Finally, brothers, we urge you in the Lord Jesus, that, as you have received instructions from us as to how you must behave to please God, so you should follow the pattern more and more. 2. For you know the instructions we gave you through the Lord Jesus; 3. For this is the will of God, even your separation from sexual immorality and that you resist fornication:*

Purity was the standard of Believers morality (transparency/pureness, innocence, integrity) *4. Each one of you must learn to control the sensual impulses that are natural in the body and do it with honor; 5. Not as the natural urge toward carnal desires as the Gentiles do in their ignorance of God: 6. None of you should be excessive and take advantage of his brother in business dealings. Because the Lord is the avenger of such excess, as our testimony forewarned you.*

Source of believer's purity *7. For God did not call us to impurity but to consecration. 8 Therefore he who rejects this instruction does not reject man but rejects the God who gave us the Holy Spirit.*

Believers must learn the lesson of love

Explanation of love *9. There is no need that I write to you concerning love for the brethren, because you have learned for yourselves God's lesson about the love we ought to show to one another.*

Expression of love *10. And indeed, you practice love toward all the brethren in Macedonia:*

Extent of love *but we beseech you, that you increase your love*

Expansion of love *more and more;*

Believers must abound in ambition and be self-supporting *11. Work at being calm and mind your own business, and work with your hands as we instructed you, 12. That you may behave honestly to those outside the fellowship,* Believers must give attention to their own business and life (enterprise, partnership, affairs).

Believers must maintain a lifestyle of witnessing, *and that you may need no one to support you.*

VI. BELIEVERS MUST ABOUND IN ASSURANCE (4:13-18)

Teaching concerning death and resurrection –a preview of death and resurrection *13. I do not want you to remain in the dark about the brethren who are asleep, that you sorrow not as others who have no hope. 14. Since we believe that Jesus died and rose again, even so those who sleep in Jesus will God bring with him. 15. This we say by the word of the Lord, that those who survive unto the coming of the Lord shall not take precedence over those who have gone to their rest.*

Dead in Christ shall rise first
A preview of death and resurrection
A promise of one glory for dead and living

A picture of the Lord's return

-a return

-a resurrection

-a rapture

-a reunion

-a reassurance

16. For the Lord Himself will descend from heaven with marching orders, with the voice of the archangel, and with the trump of God: and the dead in Christ shall rise first: 17. Then we who are alive will be snatched up suddenly together with them in the clouds, to meet the Lord in the air, and we shall be with the Lord forever. 18. Wherefore encourage one another with these words.

VII. TEACHING ABOUT CHRIST'S SECOND COMING (5:1-11)

Meaning of the Day of the Lord

As a Thief in the Night *1. You have no need that I write you about the times and the seasons of these things. 2. For you know perfectly that the day of the Lord will come as a thief in the night.*

Methods of the Day of the Lord *3. For when men say, all is quiet, all is safe, that sudden destruction comes as a woman in the travel of birth; and there is no escape.*

Message of the Day of the Lord

It examines *4. Brethren you are not living in the darkness, for the day to take you as a thief by surprise. 5. Brothers you are not in the dark because you are the children of light, and the children of the day.*

It exhorts *6. We must not sleep as others do but let us be watchful and sober. 7. Night is the time for sleeping and the drunkard's time for drinking. 8. We must remain sober as men of the daylight. We must put on the breastplate of faith and love, the helmet, which is the hope of salvation.*

It encourages *9. God has not destined us for vengeance; he means us to gain salvation through our Lord Jesus Christ, 10.*

Who died for us, that, whether we wake or sleep, we should live together with him. 11. Go on encouraging one another and building up one another's faith, as you have been doing.

Paul's Practical Imperatives *(#1-12)*

VIII. ATTITUDES OF PEOPLE AND LEADERS (5:12-22)

A.   Congregation's attitude toward leadership

1. *Know those who labor among you.*
- For their work sake.

2. *Adjust to the situation.*
- And be at peace among yourselves.

B.   Leadership's attitude toward the Congregation

3. *Admonish the disorderly*

vs14. We urge you, brothers, warn the idle,

4. *Console the fainthearted*
- comfort the faint hearted,

5. *Sustain the weak*
- support the physically weak,

6. *Be patient toward all*
- show longsuffering with all men.

IX. ATTRIBUTES OF BELIEVERS AND ASPECTS OF WORSHIP (5:15-22)

C.   Attributes displayed by Believers

7. *Be forgiving*

vs15. Be certain that no one retaliates evil for evil to any man; but always pursue that which is good, but among yourselves, and to all men.

8. <u>Be happy</u>

vs16. Rejoice evermore

9. <u>Be prayerful</u>

vs17. Pray without ceasing.

10. <u>Be thankful</u>

vs18. In everything give thanks: for this is the will of God in Christ Jesus concerning you.

D. Aspects of spiritual wordship

11. <u>Be Discerning</u>

vs19. Quench not the Spirit.

12. <u>Be open to the Word of God</u>

vs20. Despise not prophesying.

E. Aspects of Spiritual Witness

13. <u>Be sure about all things</u>

vs21. Test all things;

14. <u>Be protective</u>

- cling fast to that which is good.

15. <u>Be particular</u>

vs22. Vigorously Abstain from all appearance of evil.

X. BELIEVER'S CONSECRATION AND SEPARATION FROM THE WORLD (5:23-28)

<u>Means to Preserved Believers Blameless</u> 23. May the God of peace sanctify you completely; and I pray God that no part be lacking in your spirit and soul and body be kept blameless unto the coming of our Lord Jesus Christ.

<u>Resources</u> 24. Faithful is he who calls you**,**

<u>Value</u> who will also guarantee your worthy report.

Pray for Spiritual Leadership *25. Brethren, pray for us.*
Greet all believers with Christian love *26. Greet all the brethren with the deep emotion of Christian love (a holy kiss)*
Read the Scriptures to everyone *27. I order you under special vow of the Lord that this epistle is read to all*
Benediction. *28. May the grace of our Lord Jesus Christ remain with you! Amen*

PRIMARY "A" MESSAGE TO THE THESSALONIANS

Planting a Pristine Congregation

Paul wrote to the Thessalonians from Corinth around AD 50-51. The congregation was established the year before during a short stay of the missionary team. The Jews of Thessalonica rejected Paul's ministry of three Sabbaths in the synagogue, but the team moved to the city and the people heard the good news gladly. A New Testament congregation was born: a gathering of believers who belonged to the Lord. While on his way to Corinth, Timothy was sent to check on the condition of the new believers. When Timothy's report came that the converts were doing well, but there were some misconceptions regarding the Second Coming of Christ.

One Message in Two Parts

It is our judgment that Paul's writing to the Thessalonians was one message in two parts: "A" and "B". The content of both parts was parallel and based on the Timothy Report. Paul encouraged the believers to be steadfast in persecution specifically describing events preceding the *Parousia*. He illustrated the stability of the believer's life and encouraged converts to reject worldliness and live by moral principles. Paul both answered their misunderstandings and reviewed both the conduct of the team and the content of the preaching during their short stay in Thessalonica. It appears that piritual function of the assembled believers and their daily lifestyle.

The Text of I Thessalonians "A" Follows

Togetherness in Christ "A" 1 Thessalonians 1:1- 5

1. Paul, and Silas, and Timothy, to the church assembled at Thessalonica, in union with God the Father and the Master Jesus Christ: favor to you and peace of heart, from God our Father, and the Lord Jesus Christ. 2. We always give thanks to God for you all, without ceasing making mention of you in our prayers; 3. Remembering your faith that produced works, and love that prompted labor, and hope in the Lord Jesus Christ that brought about endurance before God and our Father; 4. Knowing beloved brethren that you have been chosen of God. 5. For our good news came not only in human speech, but also in words with innate power, and in the Holy Spirit, and crammed full of conviction, as you know what kind of men we were among you for your sake.

You became Imitators "A" 1 Thessalonians 1:6 -10

6. And you became imitators of us, and of the Master, having accepted the word on a narrow path, but with joy of the Holy Spirit: 7. So you became a model for all the believers in Macedonia and Achaia. 8. For from you echoed out the word of the Master not only in

Macedonia and Achaia, but also in every place your trust God-ward is overflowed abroad, so that we do not need to speak a word; 9. For others are telling of their own accord, what welcome you gave us, and how your turned from idols to serve the living and sincere God; 10. And to confidently wait the return of God's Son from heaven, whom he raised from a corpse, even Jesus our rescuer from the coming wrath.

Fluency of Speech "A" 1 Thessalonians 2:1-12

1. For you know, brethren, that the good effect of our entering in unto you, continues: 2. But even after cruel and unfair treatment at Philippi, with Godly fluency in speech we brought you good news with much anxiety and conflict. 3. Yet our appeal to you was not based on false or degraded thinking nor on cunning craftiness: 4. But passing God's scrutiny, he judged us fit to be entrusted with the good news: when we speak, it is not to please men, but God who examines our hearts. 5. You know that we never used the language of flattery, and God knows we never attempted to enrich ourselves: 6. For we never sought praise from you or others, when we might have been burdensome to you as apostles of Christ. 7. But we were tender among you, even as a nursing mother warmly takes pleasure in her children: 8. So affectionately longing for you, we were willing to share with you, not only the gospel of God, but also well pleased to share our lives, because you were valued by us. 9. You remember, brethren, our long and hard labor night and day, because we would not burden you for expenses, but freely preached the gospel of God unto you. 10. You are witnesses and so is God, how upright, honest and blameless was our conduct among you that believe: 11. As you know how we encouraged, comforted, and charged every one of you, as a father treats his children, 12. that you would lead a life worthy of God, who has called you unto the glory of his kingdom.

The Word of God is Truth "A" 1 Thessalonians 2:13 -16

13. This is why we give thanks to God without let up, because the word of God you heard from us, you willingly welcomed not as the words of men, but as the true word of God which sets in operation an effectual work in you that believe. 14. For you became imitators of the brothers in God's assemblies in Judaea who gathered in Christ Jesus, for you also have suffered similar things of your own tribesmen, just as they have from the Jews: 15. The men who killed the Lord Jesus and their own prophets also persecuted us. They displeased God and showed themselves the enemies of mankind; 16. Hindering us from speaking to the nations that they might be saved, they keep filling up the measure of their sins, and now God's final vengeance has fallen on them.

Satan Hindered "A" 1 Thessalonians 2:17-20

17. We brethren being orphaned from you for a short while in person, not in spirit, but desiring abundantly to see your face with great longing. 18. I, Paul, planned a journey to you more than once, but Satan put obstacles in our way. 19. For you alone are our hope, our joy, and crown of rejoicing in the presence of our Lord Jesus Christ at his coming. 20. All our pride and delight is in you.

Good Remembrance "A" 1 Thessalonians 3:1-10

1. When we could no longer bear up under the strain of separation, it seemed good to be left in Athens alone; 2. I sent Timothy, our brother, fellow laborer in the gospel of Christ and minister of God, to establish you and comfort you concerning your faith: 3. There must be no wavering because of these trials: you know that this is our appointed lot. 4. When we visited you, we told you that we must suffer tribulations; now you see it has come to pass. 5. When I could no longer endure, I sent to know your faith, lest by some means the tempter had tempted you, and our labor was unproductive. 6. But now that Timothy has returned from you and brought us good news of your faith and love, and that you always had good memory of us, desiring to see us as we also longed to see you. 7. Brethren your faith has brought us comfort in the midst of difficulties and trials. 8. For now life is worth living, if you stand fast in the Lord. 9. What thanks can we return to God for you and all the rejoicing we have because of you before God;

10. night and day we keep on praying that we might see your face and complete all that is lacking in your faith?

Strengthen your Hearts "A"

1 Thessalonians 3:11-13

11. Now may God himself and our Father, and the Lord Jesus Christ, direct our journey to you. 12. And may the Lord increase you and cause you to abound in love one toward another, and toward all men, even as we do toward you: 13. in order that he may strengthen your hearts, so you may be blameless in holiness before God, who is our Father at the coming of our Lord Jesus with all his saints.

The Will of God "A" 1 Thessalonians 4:1- 8

1. Finally brothers", we urge you in the Lord Jesus, that, as you have received instructions from us as to how you must behave to please God, so you should follow the pattern more and more. 2. For you know the instructions we gave you through the Lord Jesus; 3. For this is the will of God, even your separation from sexual immorality and that you resist fornication: 4. Each one of you must learn to control the sensual impulses that are natural in the body and do it with honor; 5. Not as the natural urge toward carnal desires as the Gentiles do in their ignorance of God: 6. None of you should be excessive, and take advantage of his brother in business dealings. Because the Lord is the avenger of such excess, as our testimony forewarned you. 7. For God did not call us to impurity but to consecration. 8 Therefore he who rejects this instruction does not reject man but rejects the God who gave us the Holy Spirit.

Learned the Lesson of Love "A"

1 Thessalonians 4:9 -12

9. There is no need that I write to you concerning love for the brethren, because you have learned for yourselves God's lesson about the love we ought to show to one another. 10. And indeed you practice love toward all the brethren in Macedonia: but we beseech you, that you increase your love more and more; 11. Work at being calm and mind your own business, and work with your hands as we instructed you, 12. That you may behave honestly to those outside the fellowship, and that you may need no one to support you.

Dead in Christ shall Rise First "A"

1 Thessalonians 4:13 -18

13. I do not want you to remain in the dark about the brethren who are asleep, that you sorrow not as others who have no hope. 14. Since we believe that Jesus died and rose again, even so those who sleep in Jesus will God bring with him. 15. This we say by the word of the Lord, that those who survive unto the coming of the Lord shall not take precedence over those who have gone to their rest. 16. For the Lord Himself will descend from heaven with marching orders, with the voice of the archangel, and with the trump of God: and the dead in Christ shall rise first: 17. Then we who are alive will be snatched up suddenly together with them in the clouds, to meet the Lord in the air, and we shall be with the Lord forever. 18. Wherefore encourage one another with these words.

As a Thief in the Night "A"

1 Thessalonians 5:1-11

1. You have no need that I write you about the times and the seasons of these things. 2. For you know perfectly that the day of the Lord will come as a thief in the night. 3. For when men say, all is quiet, all is safe, that sudden destruction comes as a woman in the travel of birth; and there is no escape. 4. Brethren you are not living in the darkness, for the day to take you as a thief by surprise. 5. Brothers you are not in the dark because you are the children of light, and the children of the day. 6. We must not sleep as others do but let us be watchful and sober. 7. Night is the time for sleeping and the drunkard's time for drinking. 8. We must remain sober as men of the daylight. We must put on the breastplate of faith and love, the helmet, which is the hope of salvation. 9. God has not destined us for vengeance; he means us to gain salvation through our Lord Jesus Christ, 10. Who died for us, that, whether we wake or sleep, we should live together with him. 11. Go on encouraging one another and building up one another's faith, as you have been doing.

Know those who Labor Among You "A"
1 Thessalonians 5:12 -15

12. We request brethren that you know those who labor among you, and are over you in the Lord, and give you special directions; 13. And respect them highly in love for their work sake. And be at peace among yourselves. 14. We urge you, brothers, warn the idle, comfort the faint hearted, support the physically weak, show longsuffering with all men. 15. Be certain that no one retaliates evil for evil to any man; but always pursue that which is good, but among yourselves, and to all men.

Hold Fast that which is Good "A"
1 Thessalonians 5:16 -22

16. Rejoice evermore. 17. Pray without ceasing. 18. In everything give thanks: for this is the will of God in Christ Jesus concerning you. 19. Quench not the Spirit. 20. Despise not prophesying. 21. Test all things; cling fast to that which is good. 22. Vigorously Abstain from all appearance of evil.

Preserved Blameless "A"
1 Thessalonians 5:23 -28

23. May the God of peace sanctify you completely; and I pray God that no part be lacking in your spirit and soul and body be kept blameless unto the coming of our Lord Jesus Christ. 24. Faithful is he who calls you, who will also guarantee your worthy report. 25. Brethren, pray for us. 26. Greet all the brethren with the deep emotion of Christian love (a holy kiss) 27. I order you under special vow of the Lord that this epistle is read to all. 28. May the grace of our Lord Jesus Christ remain with you! Amen.

SECONDARY "B" MESSAGE TO THE THESSALONIANS

The Text of 2 Thessalonians "B" Follows

Your Faith Grows Exceedingly "B"

2 Thessalonians 1:1- 6

1. Paul, and Silas and Timothy, to the believers gathered in Thessalonica in God our Father and the Lord Jesus Christ: 2. grace and peace to you from God our Father and the Lord Jesus Christ. 3. Brothers it is our duty and right to always thank God for you, because your faith grows exceedingly, and the love of everyone abounds toward each other; 4. so that we ourselves glory in you in the assembled of God for your endurance and faith in all your persecutions and trials: 5. this is proof positive of the righteous judgment of God, that you may be counted worthy of the kingdom of God, for which you also suffer: 6. since it is a righteous thing with God to inflict suffering upon those who are now troubling you;

A Believed Testimony "B"
2 Thessalonians 1: 7-12

7. You who are troubled may rest with us when the Lord Jesus is revealed from heaven with His mighty angels, 8. in flaming fire with great force and fury bringing deserved punishment on those who do not recognize God, and do not obey the good news of our Lord Jesus Christ: 9. the presence of the Lord and the glory of His power shall punish them with everlasting destruction. 10. Because our testimony among you was believed, in that day He shall come to be glorified in His saints and to be admired by all who believe. 11. Because of this we are praying constantly for you, praying that God may find you worthy of His calling and complete all the pleasure of His goodness and power of faith that works: 12. that the name of our Lord Jesus Christ may be honored in you and you in Him, according to God's favor and the Lord Jesus Christ.

Do Not Be Quickly Troubled "B"
2 Thessalonians 2:1- 5

1. By the coming of our Lord Jesus Christ and by our gathering together with Him, I implore you, 2. Do not be quickly troubled or unsettled in mind, neither by some alleged message from the Spirit, nor by rumor, nor by letter attributed to me, that the day of Christ is at hand. 3. Do not be deluded by any means: for that day will not come, except there first come a departure* and *the man of sin is exposed, the offspring of hell's everlasting punishment; 4. who opposed and exalted himself above all that is called God, or above everything revered; so that he attempts to take the seat in God's Temple proclaiming himself as God. 5. Do you remember that I told you these things when I was with you?*

> *v3 the word derived from Greek αποστασία (apostasia), meaning "departure" is used as a defection or revolt and is normally understood to mean a total desertion or departure from one's religion. It is translated here as "departure" because it is conceivable that this is the rapture of the believers (1 Thessalonians 4: 16, 17) not a revolt or rebellion against God. It is clear that Paul knew how to write "some shall depart from the faith" (1 Timothy 4:1). The KJV (1611) translated the word as "falling away" a seafaring term used to describe the casting off of a ship from shore, literally "to become gradually diminished in size." The Geneva Bible (1587); Coverdale Bible (1535) and Tyndale NT (1526) all translated αποστασία (apostasia) as "departing." Still some who do not believe in the rapture of believers see "apostasia" as a departure from religious convictions rather than the rapture of the saints.

Now You Know "B"

2 Thessalonians 2: 6 -12

6. And now you know what the restraining influence is that will be revealed on God's timetable: 7. for the secrecy of wickedness is now in operation: only He who now obstructs will continue to hinder until He be removed out of the way. 8. And then the Lawless One will be revealed, whom the Lord will consume with the word of His mouth and shall annihilate him by the radiance of His presence; 9. The Lawless One will come with the aid of Satan's influence with power and counterfeit signs and wonders; 10. and with all the delusions of unrighteousness in those who perish; because they did not receive the love of truth that they may be saved. 11. This is why God permitted a deceiving influence among them, so they give credit to falsehood; 12. that they all could be condemned who refused to believe the truth, but gave preference to disobedience

Stand Fast and Hold the Way of Life "B"
2 Thessalonians 2: 13 -17

13. Beloved of the Lord, we are obligated to always give thanks to God for you, because God from the beginning has chosen you to be saved by the consecration of the Spirit and by faith in the Truth: 14. He called you through our gospel to obtain the glory of our Lord Jesus Christ. 15. Therefore, beloved, stand fast and hold the way of life you have been taught, whether by the spoken word or by letter. 16. So may God and our Lord Jesus Christ Himself who has showed such love to us, giving us unfailing comfort and enduring hope through His grace. 17. Encourage your hearts and confirm you in all right behavior, action and speech.

The Lord is Faithful "B"
2 Thessalonians 3:1- 9

1. Finally, pray for us, that the word of the Lord may hold its onward course and be extolled and triumph, even as it did with you: 2. And that we may be preserved from wrong-headed and malicious men for all men do not have faith. 3. But the Lord is faithful, who shall strengthen you, and protect you from evil. 4. And we have assurance in the Lord concerning you, sure that you are doing and will do as we instructed you. 5. And may the Lord guide your hearts into a deeper realization of God's love and into steadfastness as you patiently wait for Christ. 6. Now we instruct you, brethren, in the name of our Lord Jesus Christ, that you shun any brother whose life is disorderly, and not after the way of life you received from us. 7. For you know how you should imitate us: for we behaved ourselves orderly among you; 8. neither did we eat without paying for it; but toiled hard night and day, that we might not be a burden to anyone: 9. not that we did not have the right of support, but to make ourselves an example for you to follow.

Be Not Weary in Well-Doing "B"
2 Thessalonians 3: 10 -18

10. When we were with you we instructed you that if any would not work, neither should they eat. 11. For we understand that some among you behave in an undisciplined manner refusing to work at all but interfere in others affairs. 12.

Now with the authority of the Lord Jesus Christ, we urge such people to attend quietly to their own affairs and earn their own living. 13. But, brethren, be not weary in well-doing. 14. And if any man obeys not the instructions of this letter, note that man, and shun him, that he may feel shame. 15. Yet do not consider him an enemy, but caution him as you would a brother. 16. And may the Lord of peace grant you peace everywhere and continually. The Lord is with you all. 17. The salutation of Paul with mine own hand, which is my signature in every letter I write. 18. The favor of our Lord Jesus Christ is with you all. Amen.

Stumble: take a quick step to keep from
falling; to make a slip, mistake or
blunder, especially a sinful one;
to stumble over a question;
to stumble and fall from grace.

10

DEVELOP Quality By Assessing Strengths And Weaknesses

— quantifying orthodoxy and orthopraxis by comparing the local congregation with the seven sample churches of Revelation.

Quantifying Orthodoxy and Orthopraxis

A sampling of New Testament Congregations is presented in the Revelation for the benefit of all the churches. Observing the strengths and weaknesses of these congregations can become a learning experience for present churchgoers. One cannot construct a superior organization until they have corrected the inferior nature of the present. The Revelation is a mysterious and almost unfathomable part of ancient scripture. While scholars have expressed personal views on the concepts and constructs presented in this chapter, they are offered here as a starting point for additional analysis.

The data presented are not considered definitive and should require further discussion. Although Revelation was written to the congregations of Asia Minor and others were asked to listen to what the Spirit was saying about the individual congregations, present-day places of worship would benefit from understanding the positive and negative points observed. This is the only part of sacred scripture that offers a blessing to those who read and/or listen to the words whether or not those words are clearly understood.

1. This is the Revelation of Jesus Christ, which God unveiled and signified by His messenger to His Slave John: to uncover to His bondservants things that must shortly come to pass; 2. who exposed the record of the word of God, and of the testimony of Jesus Christ, and of all things that he saw. 3. ***Blessed is he who reads, and they who listen to the words of this message for the future and is keeping those things written: for the time is at hand.*** *4. <u>John to the seven assemblies which are in Asia</u>: Grace be to you, and peace, from Him who is, and who was, and who is to come; and from the seven Spirits that are before His throne; 5. and from Jesus Christ, who is the Faithful Witness, and the First-Born of the dead, and the Prince of the Kings of the earth. To Him who loved us, and loosed us from our sins in His own blood, 6. and has made us a kingdom and priests unto God and His Father; to Him be glory and power unto the ages of the ages. Amen. (Revelation 1:1-6 EDNT)*

Was the Last Supper an Antecedent of the Communion Table?

15. And Jesus said, With earnest longing I have desired to eat this <u>Passover meal</u> with you before I suffer: 16. ***I will not eat this meal again until it is completely fulfilled in the kingdom of God.*** *17. <u>And He received a cup</u>*

and gave thanks, saying, Take this and share it among yourselves: 18. **for I will not drink of the fruit of the vine until the kingdom of God shall come.** *19. And taking a loaf, He gave thanks, and broke it apart, and gave to them, saying, this is My body given for you:* **this do for My memorial.** *20. Likewise, also the cup after eating, saying, This cup is the new covenant in My blood, shed for you.* (Luke 22:15-20 EDNT)

Is the Bride Ready?

5. And a voice came out of the throne, saying, Praise our God, all of His bondservants, and you who fear Him, both small and great. 6. And I heard as it were the voice of a great crowd, and as the voice of many waters, and as the voice of mighty thundering, saying, **Praise the Lord: for the Lord God omnipotent reigns. 7. Let us be glad and rejoice and give honor to Him: for the marriage day of the Lamb has come, and His bride has made herself ready.** *8. And to her was granted that she should be arrayed in fine linen, clean and white: for the fine linen is the righteousness of saints. 9. And he said to me,* **Write, blood-related are they who are called to the marriage supper of the Lamb***. (Revelation 19:5-9 EDNT)*

ALL FAITH-BASED CONGREGATIONS SHOULD MEASURE THEMSELVES BY THE CHARACTERISTICS OF THE MENORAH AND THE SEVEN ASSEMBLIES LISTED IN THE REVELATION

The seven identified faith-based congregations serve as examples of the strengths and weaknesses in both individual lifestyle and the quality of congregational life. They become samples of pristine congregations (1) existing at the time of John's writing; (2) categories of congregations and/or believers that may exist at any time in history; and/or (3) types of Faith-based groups that may exist in the Last Days. An important commonality is the strengths and weaknesses of the congregations and in the lifestyle of the people. Present-day believers may

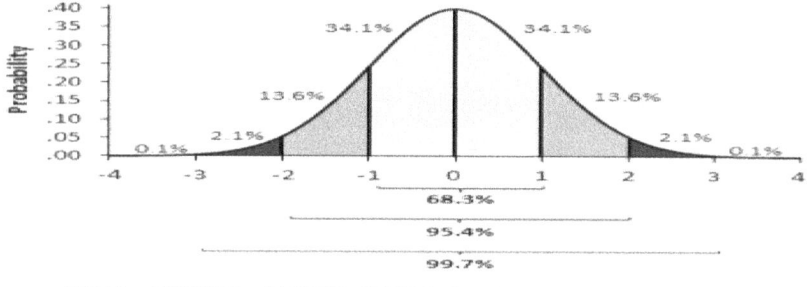

SARDUS   PERGAMOS   [LAODICEA EPHESUS THYATIRA]   SMYRNA PHILADELPHIA

learn how to correct failures and strengthen weaknesses to continue effectively on the forward path with a missional lifestyle that could expand the kingdom of God.

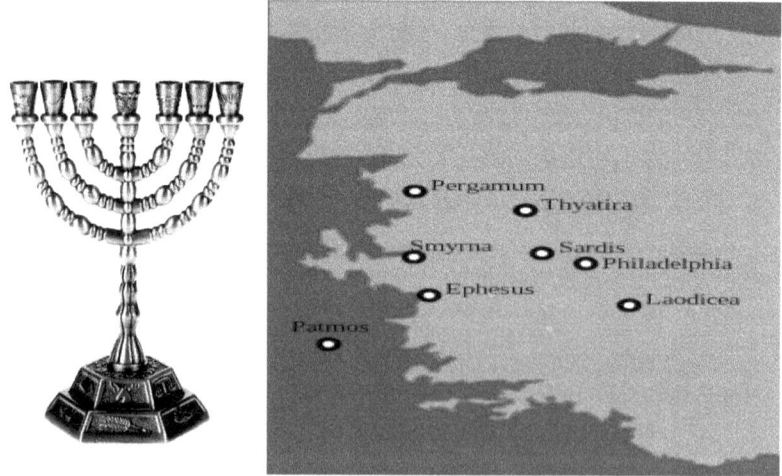

The seven congregations identified in the Revelation were located in the westernmost protrusion of Asia, which makes up the majority of modern-day Turkey. The region is bounded by the Black Sea to the north, the Mediterranean Sea to the south, and the Aegean Sea to the west. The Sea of Marmara forms a connection between the Black and Aegean Seas through the Bosporus and Dardanelles straits and separates Anatolia from Thrace on the European mainland. Anatolia is often considered to be synonymous with Asian Turkey, which comprises almost the entire country. It was called, by the Greeks, "Anatolia" (literally, *place of the rising sun*) for those lands east of Greece.

The region had been evangelized by the Apostle Paul (which included sites known from Paul's *Letters).* Under Roman rule, the land was stabilized and cities improved. The coastal communities flourished and Ephesus, especially, enjoyed great prosperity until the rise of Christianity when some infrastructure advances were neglected in anticipation of the Return of Christ.

(Compare Your Congregation with the Seven Churches -- See Appendix B)

Jesus Speaks to the Churches

John wrote, "I was in the Spirit on the Lord's Day, and I heard behind me a loud voice, as of a trumpet, saying, 'I am the Alpha and the Omega, the first and the last,' and 'What you see, write in a book and send it to the seven churches which are in Asia: to Ephesus, to Smyrna, to Pergamos, to Thyatira, to Sardis, to Philadelphia, and to Laodicea.'" (1:10-11). These churches were in the Roman province of "Asia", an area which is in western Turkey today. Chapters 2 and 3 consist of messages addressed specifically to these seven churches. Jesus says, "I know your works!" reminding them that he knows what is happening in his churches. He outlines the strengths and weaknesses of each church, warning them to steadfastly hold on to the faith which they have received. He promises great rewards to those who resist temptation, saying, "Because you have kept my command to persevere, I also will keep you from the hour of trial which shall come upon the world" (3:10). He adds, "To him who overcomes, I will give to eat of the tree of life, which is in the midst of the paradise of God" (2:7).

Although Revelation is addressed to seven churches, it is clear what Jesus said to them was meant for congregations in all times and places, for after each of the seven messages, Jesus said, *"He who has an ear, let him hear what the Spirit says to the churches."* Since these congregations are presented as an example for others, it behooves all believers to consider to the data presented in the Revelation.

I. THE CITY OF EPHESUS

Not far from the isle of Patmos on the Asian mainland was the port city of Ephesus, which was situated at the mouth of the Cayster River. It was the chief city in the region and one of the most important business and cultural centers in the Roman Empire. Although in John's time it was on the coast, it is now several miles inland due to natural changes in the coastline. The ruins have been extensively excavated. Ephesus was a prominent Christian congregation in an area served by Paul, Peter, and John, with John being the leader at the time of his exile to Patmos.

The Ephesians possibly had some pride with regard to their position of prominence, but Jesus reminds them to whom they really belong, *"These things says He who holds the seven stars in His right hand, who walks in the midst of the seven golden lampstands."* They had strayed from their original purpose, and Jesus warned, *"Repent and do the first works, or else I will come to you quickly and remove your lampstand from its place."* It appears the warning was not heeded, for despite efforts to save it, the famous port gradually silted up and Ephesus was left high and dry, cut off from the main source of its wealth. All that remains of Ephesus and the congregation are its ruins. It is not known which came first: the slow demise of the city or the rapid removal of their candlestick. One lesson here is that a city or a church are more than a place; they are people and will not last forever. Notwithstanding the predictable decay of buildings and the expected demise of people, true believers are promised eternal life.

Congregation at Ephesus
(Orthodoxy without lifestyle-love)

Jesus walking among the seven golden lampstands observed the strengths and weakness of each congregation. This scrutiny at Ephesus showed steadfast endurance and intolerance for evildoers; it revealed that the congregation had examined those who claimed to be God's messengers and found them false. Believers at Ephesus steadfastly endure and carried burdens for Christ's sake without despairing and had despised immorality; however, they had forgotten their first love which was a lifestyle of benevolent affection for both God and man. They were told to repent and return to their early lifestyle or their candlestick would be removed. Individual overcomers were promised eternal life in the Paradise of God, but there was no promise that the church at Ephesus would survive. The church perished along with the city. It takes more than orthodoxy for a people to prosper and endure as a Faith-based congregation. There must be a missional lifestyle to demonstrate and share the love of God to those outside their fellowship or the comfort zone of the congregation.

> <u>*2.I know your works, and your weariness, and your steadfast endurance, and how you cannot tolerate evil-doers: and you have tested those who say they are apostles, and are not, and found them false: 3. and have steadfastness, and have carried a heavy load for My name's sake have labored and not despaired*</u> *4. Nevertheless, I have "something" against you,* **because you have left your first love. 5. Remember therefore from where you have fallen and repent, and live as you did at first; or else I will come quickly, and remove your lampstand from its place, except you repent. 6. But this is in your favor, that you hate the deeds of the Nicolaitans,* which I also hate. 7**. *He who has an ear let him listen to what the Spirit says to the assemblies; to him who overcomes will I give to eat out of the tree of life, which is in the Paradise of God. (Revelation 2:2-7 EDNT)*

> *v6 The Nicolaitans taught that to master sensuality, one had to experience the whole range of immorality. These heretics were hated and expelled by the assembly in Ephesus but tolerated by Pergamum.

II.   CITY OF SMYRNA

About forty miles to the north of Ephesus on the coast was the city of Smyrna, the "glory of Asia." It still exists today, though it is now called Izmir. Like Ephesus, Smyrna had the double advantage of being located on a major highway and having an excellent port. Rich farmland surrounded the city, and it was a merchandising center for an inland trade route. The was destroyed earlier was little more than a village for three centuries, but revived as a business and cultural center, and had made so much progress that it rivaled Ephesus in importance. Smyrna, therefore, was known as the city that had died and come back to life. So, the opening words of Jesus were significant for the congregation **"These things say the first and the last that was dead and came to life."**

The city's leadership, as a token of Smyrna's loyalty to Rome, erected a temple to "the goddess Rome." About two hundred years later, in 26 A.D., construction began on another temple for the worship of the Roman emperor, Tiberius. The city was famous as a center of learning, particularly in the fields of science and medicine. It was also known for its architecture, especially the Temples and public buildings, which formed a crowning ring around the top of Mount Pagos.

Congregation at Smyrna
(Suffering poverty, but spiritually rich)

Jesus observed that the congregation at Smyrna was being afflicted and their God was being vilified and they were enduring a scarcity of material goods, but they were seen as being spiritually rich. They were warned of forthcoming suffering in prison to test their faith and were told to be faithful unto death and they would receive a Crown of Life. Nothing was said about the viability of the congregation itself. They were opposed to those who practiced satanic worship which included Jewish rituals. Their opposition was such that they suffered for it, even to the point that some died. This was to prove a test for a short time. There are no weaknesses pointed out in Smyrna. They were faithful even while being persecuted, to the point of death. In reference to the "crown of Smyrna," Jesus told the believers, *"Be faithful until death, and I will give you the crown of life."*

> 9. <u>I know the affliction and poverty you endure,</u> (**but you are rich**) <u>and I know the slandering and abuse from those who say they are Jews, and are not, but are the assembly of Satan.</u>
> 10. <u>Fear nothing that you may suffer: soon, the devil will throw some of you into prison, that your faith may be tested;</u> and you will have ten days of tribulation: **be faithful unto death, and I will give you the crown of life.** 11. He who has an ear let him listen to what the Spirit says to the assemblies; he that overcomes shall not experience wrong from the second death. (Revelation 2:9-11 EDNT)

III. CITY OF PERGAMOS

Pergamos was about a hundred miles north of Ephesus and situated about fifteen miles inland. There remains a small town on the site, though over the years the name has changed slightly, and it is now called Bergama. During Pergamos' time of glory a library was built which was second only to that of Alexandria. There was also a famous school of sculpture. Their affluence was tied to a number of flourishing industries, including agriculture, wool products, silver, and parchment, which was invented there. Jesus used a two-edged sword to figuratively refer to the power of words: *"He who has the sharp two-edged sword."* This was a fitting introduction for a city famous for its parchment and its library. Jesus continued, "*I know your works, and where you dwell, where Satan's throne is."* This is a reference to the **"throne of Zeus"** which was located on the top of a hill overlooking the city. Zeus, as the chief of the gods, was a particular symbol of paganism, and the city was a major center for pagan cults. In addition to Zeus, there were temples dedicated to Athena (goddess of wisdom), Apollo (god of prophecy, music and poetry), and Asclepius (god of medicine in ancient Greek religion). It also became the site of the first temple erected for the worship of Caesar, during the reign of Augustus. Some temple *"priestesses"* were actually prostitutes, used as part of their pagan worship.

Congregation at Pergamos
(Good people influenced by an evil place)

Walking among the seven golden lampstands Jesus observed the strengths and weakness of the congregation at Pergamos. The people were good but were being influenced by an evil place. In fact, their location was called the seat of Satan. It appears that evil had filtrated into the congregation from those who followed the teaching of Balaam who caused some to stray from the right path and sacrifice to idols and commit acts of immorality. Others followed the immoral teachings of the Nicolaitans.

This is the second mention of Satan's name. Their strengths include remaining faithful to Jesus, at least in name, and not denying Him even when one of their own was being martyred. But there had been compromise. The teaching of Balaam means there were some advocating liberalism to the point of sin; that is, tempting others to sin by eating meat sacrificed to idols and participating in temple rites, probably in the name of "grace" or "forgiveness." The teaching of Balaam included sending some priestesses into the Israelite camp to tempt the men into the worship idols. Balaam believed falsely that God would then destroy the Israelites. They were faithful in many things, but had allowed false teaching to enter the congregation to such a degree that it needed to be cleansed. Pergamos was faithful in much but allowed false teaching to enter and take root. The congregation was told to collectively repent quickly or a Holy War would be launched against them.

> 13. **I know where you live, a place where Satan sits enthroned: and you hold fast My name, and have not denied My faith**, *even in the days when Antipas was My faithful martyr, who was slain among you, where Satan lives.*
> 14. **But I have a few things against you,**

because you have among you those who hold the teaching of Balaam, who taught Balac to cast a stumbling block before the children of Israel, to eat things sacrificed to idols, and to commit fornication. 15. So hast thou also them that hold the teaching of the Nicolaitans, which thing I hate. *16. <u>Repent or else I will quickly come to you and make war against such men with the sword of My mouth.</u> 17. He who has an ear, let him listen to what the Spirit says to the assemblies; to him that overcomes I will give to eat of the hidden manna, and will give him a white stone, and on the stone a new name written, that no man knows saving he who receives it. (Revelations 2:13-17 EDNT)*

IV.   CITY OF THYATIRA

About eighty miles to the north of Ephesus and about fifty miles inland lay the city of Thyatira. It was not a city of great importance, but it was a commercial center, and there were a number of trade guilds. It was also a garrison town. The citizens of Thyatira were expert metalworkers known for making helmets, swords, armor, and other domestic implements. The opening remarks of Jesus dealt with *"a flame of fire and fine brass"* and He closed for this military town *"He who overcomes, and keeps my works until the end, to him I will give power over the nations."*

Unfortunately, the heathen practices common to the other cities in the area were practiced and Jesus warned, *"You allow that woman Jezebel, who calls herself a prophetess, to teach and beguile my servants to commit sexual immorality and to eat things sacrificed to idols."* Thyatira's lack of faithfulness had allowed sensuality to enter and take root within a small part of the congregation. Still overcomers were promised a new identity, but there were no such promises for the congregation at Pergamos. It becomes obvious that immorality will destroy any congregations regardless of the faith and good behavior of a few.

Congregation at Thyatira
(Active but weakened by Immorality)

Paul's first convert in Europe was "a certain woman named Lydia, a seller of purple from the city of Thyatira" (Acts 16:14), but there is no record that the city played a role in the growth of the early Christianity. Their strengths include good deeds, love, faith, service and perseverance. Their weakness, however, was that some are following a woman prophetess to encouraging some to become involved in immorality. Probably a small cult. Obviously, this woman was a regular member and may have been a part of the congregation at the time of this writing. Good people cannot worship with those who follow the teaching and lifestyle of Balaam and the Nicolaitans. (See Ephesians 5:7-13)

14. Stop being harnessed together in an alien yoke with unbelievers: for what sharing or participation has righteousness with lawlessness? And what close relationship has light with darkness? 15. And what harmony has Christ with the worthless prince of darkness? Or what can a believer share in common with an unbeliever or freethinker? 16. And what common ground can the temple of God have with idols? For

believers are the temple of the living God; as God said, I will dwell in them, walk in them, and I will be their God and they shall be my people. 17. Wherefore come out from among them and separate yourselves, says the Lord, and have no contact with impurity and I will receive you. 18. And will be a Father to you and you shall be My sons and daughters, says the Lord Almighty. (2 Corinthians 6:14-18 EDNT).

V. CITY OF SARDIS

Sardis was about fifty miles to the northeast of Ephesus. There is still a town on the site, but over the years it has come to be known as Sart. Sardis was famous for its arts and crafts. It was also the first place to mint gold and silver coins and became a legend for their riches. The story of how the Persians had overcome the supposedly invincible citadel at Sardis with a surprise attack was well-known. Hence Jesus' words: "If you will not watch, I shall come upon you as a thief, and you shall not know what hour I shall come upon you." Later Rome was the dominant power during the time the Revelation was written. Despite huge relief efforts by Rome, Sardis never recovered its former glory after it was devastated by a great earthquake in 17 A.D. The humbled town continued to exist.

Revelation is evidence that there was a Christian community there in the late first century. Jesus alluded to the diminished glory of Sardis, "I know your works, that you have a name that you are alive, and yet you are dead." The congregation and the town had a status because of a former glory which no longer existed. Jesus acknowledged the city was famous for its garment industry when He said, "overcomers will be clothed in white garments."

Congregation at Sardis

(Good reputation but about to die)

Observing the congregation at Sardis, Jesus saw a group with appeared to others to be alive, but were spiritually dead. They were told to wake up, be watchful, and strengthen the weak that were about to die. This happened because they had not been keeping their covenant relationship with God. They were warned that Jesus would come when unexpected and they would be judged for their lethargy and careless lifestyle. On a positive note, Jesus found a few who had not tarnished their purity and were worthy of a white garment and would be verified as a permanent name in the Book of Life.

1. I know your reputation that you are alive, but are dead. 2. Wake up and watch and strengthen the things that remain, that are ready to die: for I have not found your works fulfilled before God. 3. Remember what you heard and what you received as a permanent deposit, and hold fast, and repent. If therefore you will not wake up, I will come as a thief, and you will not know what hour I will come. 4. But you have a few people in Sardis who have not sullied the purity of their lives: and they will walk with Me in white: for they are worthy. 5. He who overcomes, the same will be clothed in white raiment; and I will never blot his name out of the book of the life, but I will openly confess his name before My Father, and before His angels. 6. He who has an ear let him listen to what the Spirit says to the assemblies. (Revelation 3:1-5 EDNT)

VI. CITY OF PHILADELPHIA

Philadelphia, which today is the Turkish town of Alaşehir, was about seventy miles inland from Ephesus. The name means "brotherly love." The city derived its name from its founder, a King named Philadelphia, not from a reputation for brotherly love. In addition to being an agricultural center, Philadelphia was a producer of leather goods and textiles. It also served as a commercial link between other cities. Like Sardis, Philadelphia was devastated by the earthquake of 17 A.D. Located right on the fault, it is said to have suffered after-shocks for twenty years.

Philadelphia's congregation was faithful in spite of persecution, hence Jesus' introduction: "These things say He who is holy, He who is true." Christ continues his description of himself with a quote from Isaiah: "…he who has the key of David, he who opens and no one shuts, and shuts and no one opens."

Jesus closed the message, "He who overcomes, I will make him a pillar in the temple of my God, and he shall go out no more." The congregation in Philadelphia had indeed been a pillar, surviving to the present day in spite of the advance of Islam. It can take comfort in the words of Jesus: "Because you have kept my command to persevere, I also will keep you from the hour of trial which shall come upon the world."

Congregation at Philadelphia
(Faithful but too weak to Grow)

In contrast to Sardis, Philadelphia appears to have its spiritual act together. Twice the phrase is used, "Because you have kept My word…." Again, Satan is seen as the Tempter. Their faithfulness and steadfastness in God's Word is providing an opportunity to reap a spiritual harvest.

Jesus saw the congregation at Philadelphia as having an open door that could not be closed. Although having only little strength they had kept God's Word and been faithful. These faithful few would grow strong and cause the assembly of Satan to bow down and learn of My love for you. The warning was that Jesus would come quickly and that they should hold on and let no one take their rightful crown. Jesus saw those who were true to the lessons of endurance would be safe in testing and become a pillar in the temple of God with an eternal seat at the Lord's Table.

8. I know your works: watch, I have set an open door before you, and no man can shut it: for you have a little strength, and have kept My word, and have not renounced My name. 9. Watch, I will make them of the assembly of Satan, who say they are Jews, and are not, but do lie; watch, I will make them to come and bow down at your feet, and to learn that I loved you. 10. Because you did keep true to My lesson of endurance, I also will keep you safe in the hour of testing that will come upon all the world, to test those who dwell upon the earth. 11. I come quickly: hold fast to what you have, that no man may take your crown. 12. I will make him who overcomes a pillar in the temple of My God, and he shall never leave it again: and I will write upon him the name of My God, and the name of the city of My God, that is new Jerusalem, that comes down out of heaven from My God: and I will write upon him My new name. 13. He who

has an ear let him listen to what the Spirit says to the assemblies. (Revelation 3:7-13 EDNT)

VII. CITY OF LAODICEA

Laodicea was situated about a hundred miles inland from Ephesus. The cities of Colossae and Hierapolis were neighbors. Paul wrote in his letter to the Colossians, "Now when this epistle is read among you, see that it is read also in the church of the Laodiceans and that you likewise read the epistle from Laodicea" (Col. 4:16). Unfortunately, the epistle to Laodicea which Paul mentions was not been preserved unless it became the Letter to the Ephesians.

Laodicea was also famous for its black wool, from which were made clothes and carpets, and as a center of medicine. Its eye salve was particularly famous. However, despite all of these advantages, the city was spiritually poor. In reference to those things for which it was famous, Jesus says, "I counsel you to buy from me gold refined in the fire, that you may be rich; and white garments, that you may be clothed, that the shame of your nakedness not be revealed; and anoint your eyes with eye salve, that you may see" (3:18).

Congregation at Laodicea

(Rich but Lukewarm and living in spiritual poverty)

Jesus saw the congregation at Laodicea as lukewarm and their spiritual failure made Him feel nauseous. This congregation was materialistic rich, but spiritually living in poverty. Conceited members felt they had need of nothing, yet were desolate, deprived of spiritual strength and were counseled to seek the pure gold of spirituality to cloth their shame of nakedness.

They were in desperate need of spiritual eye salve to improve their spiritual sight and accept divine correction with godly sorrow and repentance.

Laodicea had spiritual complacency of laziness created by materialism. There were no strong things noted in the record and the weakness was glaring. This was a new temptation not seen in other letters. It was secular materialism created by spiritual self-righteousness. Their faithfulness and steadfastness in God's Word provided an opportunity to reap a spiritual harvest, but they did not live what they knew. They are spiritually deceived; blind and not knowing that they are blind. Why does materialism create spiritual complacency and cause believers to become "lukewarm"? What could have been done to change this situation? It appears that Jesus saved the worst to the last for emphasis.

I know your works, that you are neither cold nor hot: I would you were cold or hot. 16. So then because you are lukewarm, and neither cold nor hot, I am about to spit you out of My mouth. 17. Because you say, I am rich, and increased with goods, and have need of nothing; yet you are unaware that you are desolate, deprived, broke, sightless, and exposed: 18. My counsel for you is to obtain from Me gold tried in the fire, that you may become rich; and white garments, that you may be clothed, and cover the shame of your nakedness; and salve to anoint your eyes so you may see. 19. As many as I love, I correct and chasten: be zealous therefore, and repent. (Revelation 3:14-19 EDNT)

It is assumed the seven congregations listed in Revelation are a sample of all congregations functioning during that period. Beginning with the largest city,

Ephesus, it appears the churches were listed in some geographical order. Data on each congregation identifies the positive and negative characteristics. It is assumed that provided these characteristics are adequately identified and understood, they could be used to classify or place current Faith-based congregations in placement-comparison with Ephesus and the Revelation list.

Researchers in different academic disciplines have found that the patterns of occurrence of different phenomena may be described by a set of related probability distributions called the Gaussian distribution or normal distribution. It has been shown that any random variable of interest that is the sum of a number of factors, each with its own probability distribution, is likely to be distributed normally. This particular form of probability frequency distribution is used to build the methodology of statistical induction for a set of methods of statistical inference termed parametric statistics. An overview of one method of this process of statistical inference is useful for understanding the logic and the degree of rigor that characterized modern formal investigations.

Induction is a system of logic by which a person may argue that some quality or attribute of a specific element is generally characteristic or representative of all such elements. Because a researcher can never be sure that the set of observed elements includes "all elements," the conclusions of inductive logic can never be proven absolutely "true;" consequently, a degree of uncertainty is always attached to the conclusion reached by this type of logic; however, assumptions may be supported, and a better understanding of the situation may be realized.

Statistical induction is a methodology, derived from the general idea of inductive logic. It bases the assessment of the degree of uncertainty that applies to an inductive conclusion on the probability of selecting sample elements that are representative of all elements in a system of interest. Typically, the characteristics that interest researchers are not present to the same degree in every part of a population. If they were, the characteristics would be randomly distributed (that is, every part would have the same chance of having the same degree) and therefore the characteristics would be would have arrangement or order and consequently of interest to researchers.

Provided the positive and negative characteristics of the sample congregations are understood, it would be possible to identify and classify (or place local congregations) into category comparison with the sample of churches in Revelation. It would be a broad classification that assumes that a certain percentage of all faith groups would be in a particular category. It would appear that 68.3% of Faith-based congregations would fall into comparison with [Laodicea; Ephesus; Thyatira]; and 95.4% of all faith-based congregation would share the characteristics of [Sardis; Pergamos; Laodicea; Ephesus; Thyatira; Smyrna; Philadelphia] with the balance falling outside the norm. Perhaps 0.1 % would be outside this norm either as grossly negative or absolutely positive. There would be no perfect congregations because they are made up of human beings!

What is true of the sample may be generalized to the whole. Just as the early disciples of Jesus were not perfect, a composite of their characteristics would create a unique but composite of ideal New Testament man. Likewise, a composite of the nature and characteristics of the sample seven assemblies of Revelation could create an ideal or amalgamated congregation. Also, present faith-based groups could assess their status by comparison with the results of the amalgamation that merged the sample into one single ideal entity. Surely it would be different, but there would be a blend or a combination of good and bad attributes. This conception would be ideal but not the real nature of the congregation. However, it would provide a guide for growth and show areas were repentance and change were needed.

Families, faith-based groups, and constituted authorities are failing their obligations. Many have forgotten that opportunity equals obligation.

11

IMPROVE Evangelism By Associating Conversion With The Human Birth Cycle

*— a process, not an event,
that enables converts to become disciples.*

Comparing New Birth with Human Birth

An early comparison of being born again with the natural birth of a human fetus came in an exchange between Jesus and Nicodemus, a member of the Jewish ruling council. Certainly, it was hard to understand. Perhaps this is one reason faith-based people have failed to seriously connect the process of conception and birth to the new birth process which comes with conversion. This failure has greatly limited efforts to mentor and coach new converts and young disciples.

> *1. There was a leader among the Jews, named Nicodemus, a member of the Jewish Council: 2. who came to Jesus by night, and said, Rabbi, we know that you are a teacher from God: for no man could do these miracles except God be with him. 3.* **Jesus answered, Truly, I say to you, Except a man be born again, he cannot see the kingdom of God.** *4. Nicodemus asked,* **How can a man be born when he is old? Can**

he enter the second time into his mother's womb, and be born? 5. Jesus answered, Truly, I say, Except a man be born of water and of the Spirit, he cannot enter the kingdom of God. 6. **That which is born by physical birth is of nature; and to be born of the Spirit is a spiritual birth.** 7<u>. Do not be astonished that I said, You must be born again. 8. The wind blows where it wishes, and you hear the sound, but cannot determine from where it comes or where it is going: so is every one that is born of the Spirit.</u> 9. **Nicodemus answered, How can these things be? 10. Jesus answered, Are you a teacher of Israel, and do not understand these things?** 11. Truly, I say, we speak what we do know, and witness to what we have seen; yet you receive not our testimony. 12. **If I have told you earthly things, and you believe not, how shall you believe, if I tell you of heavenly things?** (John 3:1-12 EDNT)

The New Birth

Why was conversion to Christianity called a "new birth" or a born-again experience? It was a Hebraism and was frequently used among the Hebrews. The Talmud uses this figure as applied to proselytes. This new birth, or being 'born again' is *'from above', is by Divine power.*

God is the source of all prosperity and blessings in the hearts of mankind. Where the heart is there will be treasures that flow in love and blessings to others. When the spirit of Jesus is in the heart, it is similar to a spring in the desert, flowing to refresh all who travel near the oasis of faith. The water of life is free to all. Peter expressed this concept when he wrote something similar to: *"This water prefigured the water of baptism through which you are now brought to safety."* (1 Peter 3:21 NEB) **The birth of a child is called the "First Sacrament" by some Christians.**

> [5] *"Before I formed you in the womb I chose you, before you were born I set you apart;* (Jeremiah 1:5 NIV)
>
> [10] *From birth I was cast on you; from my mother's womb you have been my God* (Psalm 22:10 NIV)
>
> [13] *For you created my inmost being; you knit me together in my mother's womb.* [14] *I praise you because I am fearfully and wonderfully made; your works are wonderful, I know that full well.* [15] *My frame was not hidden from you when I was made in the secret place, when I was woven together in the depths of the earth.* [16] *Your eyes saw my unformed body; all the days ordained for me were written in your book before one of them came to be.* [17] *How precious to me are your thoughts,*[a] God! How vast is the sum of them! [18] *Were I to count them, they would outnumber the grains of sand—When I awake, I am still with you.* (Psalm 139:13-18 NIV)

Children and a Garden Need Cultivating

The statement *"be fruitful and replenish the earth, and subdue it:"* (Genesis 1:28) was made by God to Adam and Eve in the Garden of Eden. This was directly related to cultivating the earth and the birthing of children. The church has been called God's farm or God's Garden and it is evident that the items of a garden are perishable and must continually be replaced. Both children and a garden require constant tending.

> 16. **You have not chosen me, but I have chosen you, and appointed you to go out and bring in fruit, and that your fruit should remain: and that you should obtain answers to your prayers to make them fruitful.** 17. These things I command you, so that you may love one another. (John 15:16-17 EDNT)

LIFE AFTER BIRTH

In a mother's womb were two babies. One asked the other:

"Do you believe in life after delivery?" The other replied,

"Why, of course. There has to be something after delivery. Maybe we are here to prepare ourselves for what we will be later."

"Nonsense" said the first. *"There is no life after delivery. What kind of life would that be?"*

The second said, *"I don't know, but there will be more light than here. Maybe we will walk with our legs and eat from our mouths. Maybe we will have other senses that we can't understand now."*

The first replied, *"That is absurd. Walking is impossible. And eating with our mouths? Ridiculous! The umbilical cord supplies nutrition and everything we need. But the umbilical cord is so short. Life after delivery is to be logically excluded."*

The second insisted, *"Well I think there is something and maybe it's different than it is here. Maybe we won't need this physical cord anymore."*

The first replied, *"Nonsense. And moreover if there is life, then why has no one ever come back from there? Delivery is the end of life, and in the after-delivery there is nothing but darkness and silence and oblivion. It takes us nowhere."*

"Well, I don't know," said the second, *"but certainly we will meet Mother and she will take care of us."*

The first replied *"Mother? You actually believe in Mother? That's laughable. If Mother exists then where is She now?"*

The second said, *"She is all around us. We are surrounded by her. We are of Her. It is in Her that we live. Without Her this world would not and could not exist."*

Said the first: *"Well I don't see Her, so it is only logical that She doesn't exist."*

To which the second replied, *"Sometimes, when you're in silence and you focus and you really listen, you can perceive Her presence, and you can hear Her loving voice, calling down from above."*

— a*ttributed to Hungarian writer* **Útmutató** *a Léleknek.*

21. A foreshadow of baptism through which you are now brought to safety, not the removal of physical stains, but a satisfying of a good conscience toward God by the resurrection of Jesus Christ. 22. He now is n the right hand of God; where the Powers in heaven are lined up under His authority. (1 Peter 3:21-22 EDNT)

"You know more than you think you do."

The long life of Benjamin Spock (1903-1998) and the popularity of his seminal book, *The Common Sense*

Book of Baby and Child Care, published in 1946 (with revisions up to 2004) by Duell, Sloan & Pearce, deals with the urgent search by parents and caregivers for assistance with the problems of growing children. Dr. Spock's first book was simple and had a straight forward message to young mothers **"You know more than you think you do."** Parents and surrogate caregivers must use their common sense in dealing with the nurturing and development of children.

Spirit's Work in Conversion

Conversion is a spiritual matter; it is not the results of human marketing or good salesmanship or psychological manipulation by well-practiced rhetoricians with financial aspirations. True conversion is not brought about by programs or gimmicks. Jesus said, *No man can come to Me, without being attracted to Me by the Father"* (John 6:44) This attraction is done by the Spirit. Conversion is an outcome of the work of the Holy Spirit that produces convicts of sin, righteousness, and judgment. This gift of faith comes as a result of a moral witness and the Word of God. Yet, human beings must never consider themselves the agent of conversion. God, the Father, is the Agent of Conversion. The Spirit and believers are utilized, but an understanding of "agency" must be clear. Agency is *"he who acts through another, acts himself."* The Spirit does the ground work and believers as agents handle personal things by lifestyle, sharing the Word and mentoring and coaching. It is, however, God the Father's action that does the saving.

> *32. And if I be lifted up from the earth, I will draw all men to Me. 33. This Jesus said, signifying the manner of His death. (John 12:32 EDNT)*

> *7. Nevertheless, I tell you the truth; this is beneficial for you that I go away: for if I go not away, the Advocate will not come to you; but if I depart, I will send Him to you 8.* ***And when He comes, the world will be convicted about sin, and convinced about unrighteousness, judgment: 9. and sinfulness, because they do not believe on Me; 10. about righteousness, because I go to My Father, and you see Me no more; 11. about judgment, because the Prince of this world is judged.*** *(John 16:8-11 EDNT)*

The construct of conviction is *to agree with the verdict.* When one hears, understands, and believes what the Word says about them, they are convicted of sin. This leads to godly sorrow with confession and a profession of faith; thus, individuals are born again and converted and made suitable for a new lifestyle.

> *13. For everyone who calls upon the name of the Lord shall be saved. 14.* ***How shall they call on Him in whom they have not learned to believe? And how shall they believe in Him of whom they have never heard? And how shall they hear without a messenger?*** *15. And how shall they proclaim, except they be sent? As it is written, Fully developed are the swift feet of those who proclaim the glad tidings of the gospel! 16.* ***But they have not all learned to obey the gospel.*** *(Romans 10:12-21 EDNT)*

Law of Reproduction

The law of reproduction is clear that each living thing reproduces copies and at time imitations of themselves. The Book of Genesis declared *"the seed is in the fruit."* It is clear in nature that each plant and animal duplicates or produces a replica of itself. Corn seed produces corn. A tulip bulb generates a tulip. From acorns, an oak tree grows. Monkeys reproduce monkeys, and elephants birth elephants. Thus, believers should logically reproduce other believers and disciples should be in the process of "making disciples." Reproduction was God's plan shared in the Garden of Eden when Adam and Eve were told, *"Be fruitful and replenish the earth."*

What Kind of Witness

When Jesus gave His followers a personal commission, they were told to make disciples wherever they journeyed. The big question which confronts us becomes obvious: what kind of believer can you reproduce? What kind of witness will you be to the lost? If they are the same as you, would they be worthy of being called *"Christ like?"* Will your children or those to whom you witness develop Jesus-like qualities or share some of the same features, qualities, or characteristics? What is your record? The growth and the strength of the faith-based movement depends on reproducing and making converts into growing disciples who become mature participants in all aspects of kingdom life.

Recently, a Hindu teenager in Trinidad asked, *"Why doesn't your religion teach reincarnation?* The answer, *"Reincarnation and regeneration are cardinal tenants of Christianity. You see, Reincarnation is a 'rebirth.' If anyone be in Christ, they are a new creation. Christianity actually settles eternal destiny of individuals while they live; perhaps your religion waits till later.*

Conversion makes Changes

17. Therefore if any man be in Christ, he is a new creation: observe, the old things have passed away; all things have become new. *18. All things are of God, who has brought us together in Himself by Jesus Christ, and has given to us the ministry of bringing people together; 19. how that God was in Christ bringing together the world to Himself, not counting their false steps and blunders against them; and* **has committed us to speak intelligent words that bring man and God together.** *20. Now seeing we are representatives for Christ, as though God did make His appeal through us: we implore you in Christ's stead, come together with God. 21. For God caused Christ to become sin for us, who knew no sin;* **that we might come into right standing with God in Christ.** *(2 Corinthians 5:17-21 EDNT)*

Combining Two Gene Pools

The Hebrew language makes clear that two becoming "one flesh" does not define the sex act, but points to the combining of two gene pools into the formation of a new body, a real person; that is a child or offspring. The Hebrew word (*basar*) means *flesh, body, living creature, or blood relation*. The Hebrew word used in Genesis 2:7 for "soul" (*nephesh*) was used for life in

Leviticus 17:11 *"The life (nephesh) of the flesh (basar) is in the blood."* The word for life is the same one used for Adam becoming a living *"soul."* The word for flesh (*basar*) is the same as Genesis 3:24 for *one flesh*. The language in Genesis *"Therefore shall a man leave his father and his mother, and shall cleave unto his wife: and they shall be one flesh (basar),"* clearly indicates that a sexual union will produce a new body, a real person, a blood relation. In conception the blood is furnished by the father's sperm and the mother's womb nurtures the unborn offspring until birth.

> *4. And Jesus answered, Have you never read that the Creator made human beings male and female, 5. continuing, For this cause shall a man leave father and mother, and shall cleave to his wife: and the two shall become one flesh.* 6. So it follows they are no more two, but one body (family). (Matthew 19:4-6 EDNT)*

> ———————
>
> *v5 "one flesh" is *sarx* which suggests a human body apart from the soul. Probably this is the bonding that comes with the first child and not only the emotional bonding of a couple when vows are physically consummated.

> *31. For this reason shall a man leave his father and mother and cleave intimately to his wife, and they shall become one new body.* 32. This is a great sacred secret: but I speak concerning Christ and the church. 33. Nevertheless let each one in particular love his wife even as himself; and the wife should look to and pay attention to her husband. (Ephesians 5:31-33 EDNT)*

*v31 A new body or "one flesh" is *sarx* which suggests a human body apart from the soul. Probably this is the bonding that comes with the first child and not only the emotional bonding of a couple when vows are physically consummated.

6. For when we were yet powerless, at God's time, Christ died for the ungodly as a finished deed. 7. One would hardly give his life for a blameless man: yet possibly instead of a good man some would be courageous enough to die. 8. But God demonstrated His love toward us, in that, while we remained sinners, Christ died for us. 9. Much. more since we are now justified by His blood, we shall be rescued from final punishment through Him. 10. For if, when we were enemies, we were changed by the death of God's Son, much more, we are being changed by His life. 11. And not only so, but we also pray and rejoice in God through our Lord Jesus Christ, by His suffering we have exchanged our old life for new life at one with God. (Romans 5:6-11 EDNT)

Conversion Identified as a New Birth

When conversion is compared with human birth one begins to understand why converts were classified as being *born again* or as a "*new birth.*" With the changes which occur in the early hours and days in the life of new converts, the concept and construct of being "born again" becomes obvious. When the "new birth" is compared with conception, fetus attachment, development, and live birth of a child, the series of actions or steps required to achieve spiritual conversion and maturity are better understood. Provided the timeframe of the weeks, months and years of human development are transliterated into days and months of development for the convert, the growing in grace and knowledge by young converts, the logical steps in growing mature disciples would be easily seen. A brief study of conception, early germinal process, embryonic period of womb developing, and the fetal timetable for final viability outside the womb could bring clarity to the responsibility of family, soul-winners, church leaders, and the band of believers *belonging to the Lord* toward new converts and young and growing disciples.

The Process of Human Conception

1. **Ovulation: egg to embryo** --Monthly most mature females release one or more reproductive cells and with the physical contact of a male seed, the process of conception begins. The moment a male seed penetrates a mature egg and the fertilized egg is implanted in the tissue lining of the uterus, a state of pregnancy exists. It takes about 3 to 4 days for the fertilized egg to attach or implant itself in the uterine wall.

2. **Fetal Development: Pregnancy** --A special hormone is produced which will form the *placenta* and the *embryo*. The Mother's blood will show this hormone in about one week. The heartbeat begins during the fifth week of development. At the eighth week, the developing *embryo* is called a *fetus*. The *fetus* is considered an unborn human baby eight weeks after conception.

3. **A Long Journey** --Pregnancy is a long ten-month journey of about 40 weeks counting from the first day of the last menstrual period or about two weeks before conception occurs. The process is divided into three trimesters each lasting between 12 and 13 weeks. Changes take place during each of these periods.
    - The **germinal** period –early stage.
    - The **embryonic** period –growing and developing in the womb.
    - The **fetal** period –final development for viability outside the womb.

Remedial and Surrogate Nurturing

In research to produce a textbook for a graduate program in Family Life Education, several factors about human development (0-20) were learned that have a direct correlation to faith-based conversion and discipleship. A second edition of the textbook was published (2013) ISBN 978-19355-434-48-1 and meets the criteria for academic credit for Family Life Education courses that require NCFR Criteria # 3. Similar to footprints each child is different and all guidance becomes an individual matter. The young are gifts from God and a legacy for families, the church and the nation: therefore, nurturing skills are an essential aspect of human cultural development. This work was designed to be guidance for remedial human development (0-20) for parents, teachers, childcare workers in the public arena and those working with the young in faith-based operations.

Provided one studies the New Testament, they would discover that Jesus was nurtured and cared for by Mary and Joseph until he was 12 years old. Jesus reached a level of natural development with a knowledge base and a degree of spiritual formation based on parental instruction and traditional Jewish guidance, sufficient to feel a need to become involved in spiritual matters by age 12 concerning His "Father's business." Are parents and present faith-based groups sufficiently preparing children to participate in kingdom work?

Developmental Stages

These development stages begin with the womb because a child learns a great deal prior to birth. Sounds, the mother's emotions, even the mother's diet and habits influence the physical health and spiritual development of a child in utero. In fact, the logical development of a child begins in the lives of both parents prior to conception. At conception the gene pools of both parents are combined into one entity and the child will have DNA with traceable traits to parents and grandparents. When a child is born, a special human being enters the world, one that is different from all others that has ever or will ever walk this planet. Just as fingerprints and footprints; each child is different! Children are constructed from a gene pool that imprints their nature and are placed in an environment that influences their behavior. Children and converts will develop in stages in a negative or positive direction depending on the weight and nature of nurturing during each phase.

Steps in Child Development

1. Womb to age 3 –essential human bonding: affection, attachment, connection, relationships.
2. Womb to age 5 –basic elements of personality: behavior, disposition, and temperament.
3. Womb to age 7– layers for a knowledge base: awareness, understanding, learning, and education.
4. Womb to age 9 –rudimentary steps in character: moral integrity, correct behavior, and moral lifestyle.
5. Womb to age 11–keys to spiritual formation with continuing response to God's grace and the Holy Spirit's presence conforming one to Jesus in a community of faith, for the glory of God and for the salvation of the world.
6. Age 12–14 –peers influence more than adults: growing out of range of adult guidance; *this is why it is urgent to work with the young.*
7. Age 15–18 –other adults influence their conduct and career more than parents, teachers, or spiritual advisors.
8. (Age 19 +) --Stop the world I want to get off! At this point the maturing adult requires a secure family and spiritual anchor. *A second chance for their life to be what God intended.*

Changing Age to Months for Convert Development

1. **Conversion through 3 months** –essential spiritual bonding: affection, attachment,

connection, and new social and moral relationships.

2. **Conversion through 5 months** –basic elements of lifestyle behavior, disposition, and temperament changes.

3. **Conversion through 7 months** – first layers for a Biblical knowledge base: awareness and responsibilities, understanding of morality, learning and education.

4. **Conversion through 9 months** –rudimentary steps in Christian character: moral integrity, righteousness, correct behavior, and moral lifestyle.

5. **Conversion through 11 months*** –keys to spiritual formation with continuing response to God's grace and the Holy Spirit's presence conforming one to Jesus in a community of faith, for the glory of God and for the salvation of the world.

6. **Twelves to fourteen months after** conversion –learning to handle negative peers influence and lessening the mistrust of spiritual leaders: accepting spiritual guidance; *this is why it is urgent to work early and continuously with new converts before old friends lead them astray.*

7. **Fifteen to eighteen months following conversion** –other adults begin to influence conduct and career more than family. An urgent time for spiritual mentoring and coaching.

8. During **the six months before the two-year anniversary of conversion** –around this time,

family and close friends have a second-chance to influence behavior and future lifestyle provided they have been involved in the converts life during the past 18 months. By the two-year mark, converts and new members need a secure family and spiritual anchor in a Faith-based fellowship. *This six (6) months period is the opportunity (provided the teaching and training has been effective) for complete participation in the life of the church for their involvement and missional lifestyle to become what God intended it to be.*

---

*5. Remember, it took Saul and Barnabas one whole year (365 days) to prepare converts adequately to be recognized as true disciples by the general public. Making disciples is not an easy or swift process; it is at least a one-year project for multiple spiritual mentors and coaches.

The Old Testament recorded data about children promised to childless women. God does not do things by accident, there must be meaning in the record of performance of these promises. Observe the chronologically.

1. Isaac was promised to Sarah and Abraham (Genesis 21-22)
2. Samuel was promised to Hannah and Elkanah (1 Samuel 1)
3. John was promised to Elizabeth and Zacharias (Luke 1:5-1)
4. Jesus was promised to Mary and Joseph. (Luke 1:5-56)

Isaac was a Son of Promise

Isaac was promised to Abraham and Sarah when Abraham presented a case to God about his lack of a legitimate heir. And God said, *"Your own son will be your heir."* Both Sarah and Abraham were old beyond child-bearing age. When Sarah heard the news, she could not believe it, because she knew she was physically too old for child bearing. Yet, when God promises; it will happen. The birth of Isaac generated great faith in Abraham and this faith would be tested. When Isaac was 12 years old, God tested Abraham's faith by asking that Isaac be given completely to God as an act of obedience. Abraham learned that faith was better than questioning God and that obedience was better than sacrifice. When Abraham demonstrated his willingness to follow God's instruction: a sacrifice was provided and Isaac remained Abraham's heir. God had promised Abraham that Isaac was his heir and his descendants would cover the earth. This could never happen if his heir died at age twelve. Life is not always easy, but understanding and following the will of God is the best way forward. This is the key that unlocks human progress and spiritual growth. Abraham's response to this life-changing event brings to mind a statement of a martyred missionary, who wrote: *"He is no fool who gives up what he cannot keep to gain what he cannot lose." –Jim Elliot (1956)*

Hannah was Promised a Son

Prayer and faith brought Samuel into Hannah's life. She was barren and desperately wanted a son. She continually asked God to take away her reproach and promised to *"give the child back to God for his whole life."*

Her husband, Elkanah was supportive and this fulfilled God's requirement that a child have both a mother and a father. In the allotted time a son was born and named, Samuel, and as soon as he was weaned he was given to God for the rest of his days. This did not mean abandonment by his parents. Elkanah offered support in the early days and was faithful when Samuel was weaned by traveling with Hannah to Jerusalem to make good Hannah's promise.

This is a story of sadness and frustration about a woman who had no children. She went to the Tabernacle and prayed earnestly for a son and promised to give him back to the Lord *"all the days of his life."* Her name was Hannah and her husband was Elkanah. As recorded in (1 Samuel 1) after an earnest prayer to God for a son, she was convinced that God would give her a son. She was no longer sad. She discussed the matter with her husband and they decided (1 Sam 1:19) to go early the next morning to the Tabernacle and worship before the Lord and return home. In the course of time Hannah conceived and gave birth to a son. The child was named Samuel because Hannah had prayed for God to open her womb and give her a son. The next time her husband made his annual visit to the Tabernacle at Shiloh, Hannah decided not to go until the child was weaned and Elkanah agreed.

As soon as Samuel was weaned, his parents took him to Shiloh and presented him to Eli, the Priest. Hannah reminded Eli, That she was the woman downcast and praying for a son and you her that God would answer her prayer. The child has been weaned and I am giving him to the Lord for as long as he lives. *"And she left him there at the Tabernacle for the Lord to use."* Hannah and Elkanah returned home without Samuel and he became the Lord's helper, for he assisted Eli the priest. And the boy Samuel continued to grow in stature and in favor with the Lord and with men.

The story of Samuel's early development was not over. From conception to birth was the normal time frame; however, Samuel's presentation at the Tabernacle was not clear. The weaning process took from 2 to 5 years. Then the small boy was to be trained by Eli as his assistant. Eli taught Samuel to listen when God spoke. Three times God spoke to Samuel and he thought it was Eli calling him, but Eli explained it is the Lord, *"When God speaks to you again, listen!"* This Samuel did and became a great prophet and all Israel listened to him.

> *The Lord was with Samuel as he grew up, and he let none of God's words fall to the ground, and he was attested as a prophet of the Lord. The Lord continued to appear at Shiloh, and there he revealed himself to Samuel through His word. (1 Samuel 3:19-21 NIV)*

God was not through with the birth mother and father. When Samuel ministered before the Lord as a boy wearing a linen ephod, he was learning. Annually his mother made him a little robe and took it to him when she and her husband went to worship. Each year Eli would bless the family and ask God to give them other children: Hannah later birthed three sons and two daughters. And Samuel grew up in the service of the Lord. The author sees a pattern in the story of Hannah that relates directly to conversion and early discipleship training for the present band of believers.

First, there was a desire for a child and earnest prayers for God to intervene in the process. It appears that the couple were living together in a normal fashion without expecting or desiring a child. Perhaps Hannah developed a dissatisfaction with leaving the birthing and raising of children to others and felt left out of the childbearing process. To be childless was a disgrace among women of her day. This required urgent but simple an *"Ask and you will receive"* prayer. Then the husband was told of God's promise and he accepted by faith and it worked: God opened the womb of Hannah and she conceived and bear a son, Samuel.

Next, there was a decision made between mother and father. When it came time for their annual journey to the Tabernacle to worship, Hannah felt she must care intimately for the child until he was weaned, and the father agreed. From conception to birth there was anticipation; from birth to weaning there was bonding and a Divine Nurturing Attribute, a kind of spiritual DNA placed in the nurturing process that bound Hannah to Samuel. Then she remembered: a promise to give him to the Lord all the days of his life. The parents agreed that when the child was weaned, they would take him to the Tabernacle for Eli to train for the Lord's service.

The weaning of a child according to Jewish tradition was from 24 months to 5 years based on the maturity of the child and the discretion of parents. An exact age at which Samuel entered the Tabernacle cannot be determined. We only know he was a small boy left by his parents in the care of spiritual leaders. He was not abandoned; he was loved and cared for by his parents and trained for a lifetime of spiritual services by mature leaders which he faithfully fulfilled the rest of his life.

When the parents took the small child to Eli after weaning, it was evidence the child had survived the fragile stage of infancy and could eat solid food rather than surviving only on Mother's milk. Once weaned, Samuel could be cared for and trained by mature persons at the Tabernacle. He was now in the hands of surrogate parents for nurturing, teaching and the training process required to prepare Samuel for his spiritual work. Eli accepted the priestly and surrogate responsibility to train Samuel and Eli taught him to "listen" to God.

Yet, Hannah, his mother was still involved in his life. Each year, stich by stich, Hannah made Samuel a little robe to wear, just like Eli's. Each year it was made a little larger and presented filled with spiritual DNA from a mother's heart and the full blessings of God. Samuel served God his whole life and when he died all Israel assembled and mourned for him and they buried him in his house in Ramah. He was finally home!

Perhaps the story of Hannah and Samuel is one reason that the New Testament conversion and discipleship was understood to be similar to the birth and growth of a child. The Church, often considered as the future Bride of Christ, must learn and participate in the "mothering" of converts and assisting their growth into mature disciples. Meanwhile, the families and the leaders of worship and faith-based education ought to pay close attention to the process of conversion and the responsibility of "making disciples" as the routine process of family life and spiritual growth to prepare the young for both present and future service to the Kingdom of God.

Believers should not neglect the truth recorded in sacred scripture. God's intervention in family matters and the upbringing of children were included and preserved for the benefit of the whole human race.

John was promised to Elizabeth and Zacharias

For many years this couple had prayed for a child, now they were too old to hope for a son. Zacharias entered the Temple to burn incense and a heavenly messenger spoke to him *"Do not be afraid the prayer you no longer pray God heard: your wife Elizabeth shall bear a son and you shall call him John."*

Zacharias and Elizabeth had stopped praying for a son, but God had already heard their prayers of the past years. Perhaps we should learn the lesson that God hears each prayer even if we stop asking because the answer is delayed. John was born and continued to grow and became strong in spirit until he entered his public ministry to prepare the way for Jesus. The rest of the story is recorded in (Luke 1:5f)

Jesus was promised to Mary and Joseph

God sent the angel Gabriel to Nazareth, a town of Galilee, 27. to a maiden named Mary engaged to a man named Joseph, of the house of David. 28. And the angel came and said, **Greetings, you are endowed with grace, the Lord is with you.** *29. And when she saw him; she was distressed at his saying, and began to reason what the greeting could mean. 30. And the angel said, Do not be afraid, Mary: for you have received the absolute loving-kindness of God. 31. And, behold, your womb shall* *conceive, and bear a son, and you shall call His name Jesus. 32. He shall be well-known, and be called the Son of the Highest: and the Lord God shall give Him the throne of His forefather David: 33. And He shall reign over the house of Jacob forever; and His reign shall have no end. 34. Then Mary asked the angel, how shall this be since I have not accepted a man? 35. And the angel answered, the power of the Holy Spirit shall come and overshadow you; therefore, the child born of you shall be called the Son of God.* (Luke 1:26-38 EDNT)

An Eye-witness and Original Disciple of Jesus

24. This is the disciple who witnessed these things, and wrote these things: and his witness is true. 25. **There are many other things that Jesus did, and if they all were written, I suppose that even the world itself could not hold the books that would be written. Amen.** *(John 21:242-25 EDNT)*

Paul's instruction to Timothy, who was still developing and maturing in the Faith, should make all believers aware of the value of Biblical teachings. In the last days of Paul's life, he referred to the Old Testament and the current letters that were circulated among the early congregations as inspired scripture. Paul claimed that the foundations of God were standing firm on the written Word. When he was concerned about spiritual maturity and future leadership, he included both chronological and spiritual maturity in the list of qualifications for leaders. Reminding Timothy not to advance a novice or a new convert before they learned the basics of faith and developed an appropriate lifestyle. He reminded Timothy of the value of sacred writings that were inspired by the Spirit…

> *…must be one who is a good head of his own family and keeps his children in order by winning their full respect; 5. if a man has not learned how to manage his own household, will he know how to govern God's church? 6.* ***Not a recent convert,*** *lest being puffed up he fall into judgment of the devil. 7. Moreover he must have* ***a good report from those outside the church; that he not falls into reproach and into the snare of the devil.*** *(1 Timothy 3:4-7 EDNT)*

> *14. Remind them of these things, solemnly witnessing before God not to fight with words, for they are not useful but bring destruction to the ones hearing. 15.* ***Be eager to present yourself approved to God, a workman unashamed, cutting straight the word of truth.*** *(2 Timothy 2:14-15 EDNT)*

> *14. But continue to hold fast the things you have learned and been convinced of, knowing the teachers from whom you learned them; 15. and from early childhood you have known the sacred letters, the ones able to make you wise unto salvation through faith in Christ Jesus.* ***16. All sacred writings are God-breathed, and serviceable for teaching, for warning, for correction, for instruction in righteousness, 17. in order that the man of God may be***

> ***adequately equipped for every good work***. *(2 Timothy 3:14-17 EDNT)*

Peter, as an eye-witness, in the last phase of his life wrote plainly about the same matter:

> *15. Moreover, I will make it my endeavor that after my departure you will **always remember these things**. 16. For we have not pursued deceitfully developed allegories, but were eyewitnesses to His majesty when we made known to you the power and presence of our Lord Jesus Christ. 17. For He received from God the Father honor and glory, when a voice came from the magnificent glory This is My Son, My beloved in whom I am delighted. 18. And we His companions on the holy mountain heard this voice coming from heaven. 19. **So this makes the word of the prophets more certain for us: and you do well taking heed, as to a lamp shining in a gloomy place, until the day dawns and the morning star shines in your hearts; 20. Knowing this firstly, that no prophecy of scripture becomes its own solution. 21. For no prophecy was brought forth by the will of man at any time: but men spoke from God being brought forth by the Holy Spirit.*** *(2 Peter 1:15-21 EDNT)*

Present-day converts are adopted into the Family of God. The current believers must not only serve as enablers for these new souls, they must become remedial and surrogate parents nurturing their growth and development.

God ordained and ordered three basic institutions for the good of individuals. These three primary entities are interrelated and cannot survive alone. A philosophy of life begins with an awareness of these basic institutions that were intended and structured by Divine Providence for the benefit of the human race. They are the **nuclear family**, **formally constituted community**, and **faith-based entities**.

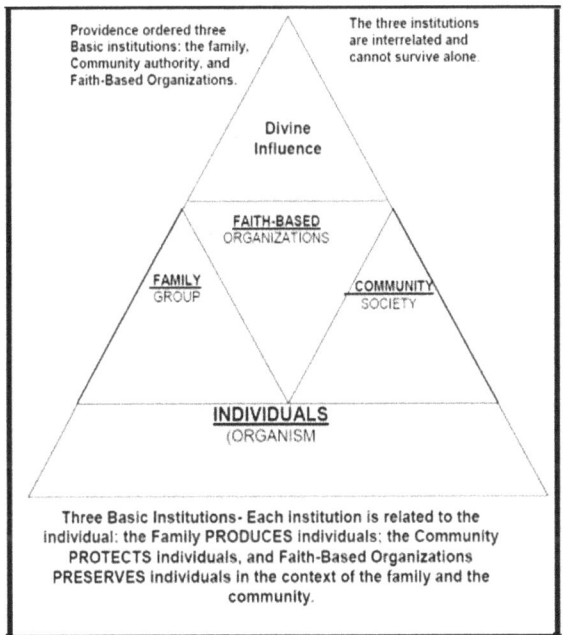

These three primary entities are interrelated and cannot survive alone. Providence designed the physical makeup of human beings so that individuals would be produced within an established nuclear family, protected in a formally, constituted community, and preserved in the context of both family and community through the guidance of a faith-based entity. Those who care about the human race and the institutions designed to produce, protect and preserved individuals must clearly comprehend that the primary concern of Providence in establishing these basic institutions was the welfare of individuals. When rights and justice are placed on the back burner in order to increase the free-time of dysfunctional parents, God's intended purpose is thwarted. When institutions function for the benefit of a few their purpose is neglected. Individuals must never become just a number to be discarded or dealt with arbitrarily. Of course, there are times when behavior violates rules of ethics and culture and eliminates individuals from the productive elements of society.

In such case, the entity must function for the good of the whole. The **nuclear family** is a basic social unit consisting of parents and their children living in one household and connected to an extended family by a kindship relationship. Some present families are scattered across the world seeking relief, recreation, and retirement. When children are born without the care and nurture of a loving two-parent family and grow up in an immoral and indifferent community without the influence of a Faith-based environment, many problems are inflicted on society because of defiled and dysfunctional individuals. These difficulties complicate the cure and care of souls.

A **formally constituted community** is a group of people gathered in a neighborhood and linked by similarity, kinship, and identity. Within the pluralistic society, neighborhoods are mixed, ethnic groups intermarry, children are born out of wedlock, and some are left abandoned, neglected or abused without parental guidance or community support. It has become difficult for the extended family to care for all the unsupported children whose carefree, sick, or overwhelmed individuals have gone their own way and left the responsibility to parents, grandparents or other members of the community.

In the effort to protect individuals, the community often protects the guilty from the wrath of others. Yet, the community is structured to punish individuals who violate the conventional wisdom and community authority but does little to correct the dysfunctional family unit that neglects or abuses the children. Why are those who abandon children not punished to the fullest extent of the law? Why are parents not required to financially support their children or pay for the support others must provide? An ordered society must consider both the protection of the individual and the separation of those who would harm the family and community. There was a time when Faith-based groups handled lots of these problems, but gradually these opportunities to serve the needs of others was handed over to governments and secular agencies. Some are dismissive of the community and snub their nose at a moral society, but little is done to correct the problem. Why must a few pick up the broken pieces and pay the bill for the support and care of the neglected?

A **Faith-based Entity** is a group of kindred souls identified by common beliefs and moral structure. The mobility of society and the immorality of the people have jeopardized the influence of Faith-based organizations. All of this leaves some individuals bearing the burden of family dysfunction, community breakdown, and society's failures due to the lack of moral leadership and honorable elected servants. By default, some individuals, a few socially responsible companies, and Faith-based entities have established places of refuge and entities for childcare that includes both practical education and spiritual edification.

A Case for Individual Care

Historically, one can clearly see divine intervention and lovingly arranged care, support, and nurturing of families and children. The fact that it takes two to biologically conceive a child is evidence that the Creator intended both mother and father to be involved in the bringing up of a child. A child was to be produced, sheltered, and nurtured in a nuclear family, protected, developed in a constituted community, and preserved in the context of both family and community under the influence of Faith-based entities to be adequately prepared to make a contribution to society. The intention was to make individuals moral citizens of the community and prepare them to become mystical citizens of heaven.

God Does Not Have a PLAN "B"

Some women's rights advocates are willing to abort a child any time between conception and delivery. Since New Birth is related to the physical birth of a child, anything that hinders the process of fulfilling Jesus' command to "catch men alive" or become "fishers of men" is similar to delaying or aborting a conversion. Anything done to offend a new convert that would discourage and cause them to stumble would relate to live birth or to spiritual infanticide.

12

ENHANCE Believers Discipleship Training Using Knowledge Of Human Development

– education that reflects generic New Testament values and faith-based lifestyles.

Jesus is the Best Example

At age 12, Jesus said, "*I must be about My Father's business?*" This was evidence of good upbringing by Mary and Joseph. Jesus began sharing with others His knowledge of God's plan of redemption for mankind. It was clear from scripture that Jesus continued submisive to the authority of Mary and Joseph and grew and developed under their care from age 12 until the beginning of a public ministry.

> *50. His words seemed strange to them. 51. And He went down with them and came to Nazareth, and submitted to their authority, but His mother kept all these sayings in her heart. 52*. **And Jesus increased in wisdom and stature, and in favor with God and man.** *(Luke 2:59b-52 EDNT)*

Notice the four stages of development after age 12:

1. **Wisdom** – development based on experience, knowledge, and good judgment.
2. **Stature** – a natural and expected physical development.
3. **Favor with God** – approval of behavior by God, support in spiritual matters.
4. **Favor with man** – honest and moral behavior in the sight of others.

Remedial and Surrogate Nurturing

General nurturing skills relate directly to the discipleship process. Remember the definition of parenting: the experiences, skills, qualities, and responsibilities involved in being a guardian and in teaching and/or caring for the young. Parents are the primary teachers for children and early adolescents. Most of the early knowledge base of children is founded on the guidance of parents, caregivers, and early teachers. Nurturing as well as educating requires both maternal and paternal natural instincts even if there is only one person available to do the work. The experience of a younger sister, speaks to this issue. She is an octogenarian poet:

ON FATHER'S DAY I THINK OF MOTHER

I WAS FIVE MONTHS OLD WHEN HE LEFT ME.
    HE DIED DURING THE NIGHT.
HE CAME HOME FROM A CHURCH MEETING,
    HUNG HIS CLOTHES ON A CHAIR,
WENT TO BED AND DROPPED INTO SLEEP.
    HIS HEART STOPPED BEATING WHILE HE SLEPT.
THE BIRTH DEFECT OF A LEAKY HEART VALVE

KEPT ON BEATING AS LONG AS IT COULD...
THIRTEEN YEARS BEYOND THE DOCTOR'S PREDICTION.
MY HEART DID NOT UNDERSTAND HIS ABSENCE.

WHILE GROWING UP, I ENVIED MY FRIENDS
    WHO HAD VISIBLE FATHERS.
WHY CAN'T I HAVE A FATHER IN MY HOUSE?
    MOTHER TRIED TO EXPLAIN IT IN MEDICAL TERMS.
MY SISTER AND BROTHER HAD CLEAR MEMORIES OF HIM.
    I HAD ONLY AN EMPTY SPACE IN MY MEMORIES.
WOULD I BE DIFFERENT IF HE HAD BEEN AROUND
    WHEN I NEEDED A SHOULDER TO CRY ON
OR A STRONG HAND TO GUIDE ME OVER LIFE'S BUMPS?
    I HAVE NO WAY OF KNOWING THE ANSWER.

MY MOTHER DID HER BEST TO FULFILL
    BOTH PARENTAL ROLES IN MY LIFE.
SHE WAS A MODEL OF PERSEVERANCE.
    SHE MADE CERTAIN THAT MY FATHER'S
EXTENDED FAMILY REMAINED CLOSE TO US.
    SHE COULD REPAIR MOST ANY SMALL HOUSEHOLD
PROBLEM THAT NEEDED A STRONG HAND.
    HER HAMMER, SCREWDRIVER AND PLIERS
OFTEN SAVED US A MAINTENANCE BILL.
    THANK YOU, MOTHER, FOR FATHERING ME.
ON FATHER'S DAY, I THINK OF MOTHER.

— Susanne Faust (6/2018)

A good example of a man having both the nurturing of a mother and the discipline of a father is made clear in the life and letters of St. Paul. In First Thessalonians 2:7,8 (EDNT) Paul wrote of his maternal affection,

> "We were tender among you, even **as a nursing mother warmly takes pleasure in**

> **her children;** *so affectionately longing for you, we were willing to share with you, not only the gospel of God, but also well pleased to share our lives, because you were valued by us."*

Then verses 11,12 (EDNT) Paul wrote of his paternal concern,

> *"As you know how we encouraged, comforted, and charged every one of you,* **as a father treats his children,** *that you would lead a life worthy of God, who has called you unto the glory of His kingdom."*

Shepherds and Fences

Since such a great leader of pristine Christianity could be both mother and father to young converts, surely those seeking to make disciples of young converts can allow both maternal and paternal instincts to function in producing care, comfort, and discipline for young converts who are growing in grace and knowledge. Young converts are much like sheep: they need both a shepherd to guide them toward green pastures and fences to establish boundaries as they walk through the valley and shadows of evil that will keep them on the *"straight and narrow way."*

Traveling by train from London to Birmingham, England, many sheep were grazing in pastureland along the railway. My knowledge of sheep was limited to the facts in the Bible. The only thing known was that sheep needed a shepherd. Seeing many sheep, but no shepherds, an English traveling companion was asked, *"Are the shepherds on strike?"* The answer was firm and clear: *"We don't have shepherds; we have fences."*

With this knowledge, my understanding of sheep was greatly expanded. Sheep must have either a shepherd or a fence or perhaps both. The young need both the care and direction of a shepherd and the parental or custodial restrictions of fences and rules!

> ***Note:*** the balance of this chapter [SECTION ONE – EIGHT] provides data that may be applied to new converts and new members of a faith-based group. Parents, pastors, teachers, mentors and spiritual coaches should read this section and at each point determine how the facts of development could be applied to converts, disciple-making and the timetable for growing in grace and knowledge of new folk to enable them to assume a productive role in missional discipleship. The task of dealing with the young, new converts or new people in the congregation could be made more effective and efficient provided this adaptation were made personally by each caregiver. The process of analysis and application to the task is more meaningful when completed by the care-giver.

USE SPACE FOR NOTES

SECTION ONE
(Conversion to 3 Months)

Essential Spiritual Bonding

Essential human bonding occurs in the womb and until age three. Spiritual bonding is a special intimacy that develops between soul-winners, teachers and all who establish examples of walking the right path. A new convert and spiritual mentors or coaches have special work to do from the point of conviction of sin by the Holy Spirit until about three months following a profession of faith. This time is as essential to spiritual bonding as is the human bonding to a child. Spiritual bonding should grow into an attachment and friendship with the mentor and with Jesus. This is an intimacy that happens when one grows in grace and knowledge of Jesus as a believer.

> *15. I no longer call you (servants) bond-slaves; because a bond-slave does not know what his Lord does: but you I have **called friends**; for all things that I have heard of my Father I have made known to you. 16. You have not chosen me, but I have chosen you, and appointed you to go out and bring in fruit, and that your fruit should remain: and that you should obtain answers to your prayers to make them fruitful. 17. These things I command*

you, so that you may love one another. (John 15:15-17 EDNT)

This bonding is tremendously important to the converts growth and development as a disciple. For most the initial bonding relationship will influence their future relationship issues. If the bond between the caregiver and the convert is one of love and security, they are more likely to seek out these healthy elements in future relationships. Converts who miss spiritual bonding with other believers may grow up without the capacity for love and intimacy; therefore, bonding is the first and foremost responsibility of a custodial mentor or spiritual coach when new converts or new members are placed in their care.

The Process of Bonding

Mentors and coaches should begin working with potential converts prior to their actual conversion. This ground work is vital to future growth and development into disciples. When this is missing before conversion, "the sooner the better" is the rule for the remedial bonding process to begin. Early on introduce the convert to teachers and leaders with whom they will become associated in the future. All must be comfortable with new comers regardless of whether they are converts or new members. If possible, permit the new person to make choices as to the class and teacher with whom they will associate in the early days following conversion.

When traveling and not responsible for a Sunday pulpit, my wife and I normally attend the service closest to where we sleep. One Christmas season we arrived as a visitor to a service that had a large sign up front, *"The hanging of the Greens!"* It struck us as amusing since we were "the greens." A local parishioner saw our smiles and inquired. After the *"We are the Greens"* the lady shared about her daughter who married a man named Comers. My daughter and husband are usually late everywhere they go. They moved to St. Louis and attended a new church. Yes, they arrived late. As they entered the sanctuary, the worship leader said, *"The ushers may now seat the late comers."* My daughter asked, *"Did they know we were coming?"* The lady with a big smile said, *"They were the late Comers and they were **late**!"*

    Caregivers must realize that a lack of previous parental bonding may have a lasting effect on an individual. They may become more anxious and insecure. However, a loving relationship that removes stress and provides secure surroundings will generate a sense of security and less emotional response to the situation. However, mentors and coaches should remember that some new folk do not want too much "mothering" they simply desire friends. Attempted over-bonding becomes a negative influence on growth and development.

How to Recognize Bonding

Since conversion is a "new birth" all mentors and coaches of converts and young disciples should review the signs for mutual bonding to assess the level of connection with new folk. The level of bonding is manifested by both attitude and interest. If there is discomfort, back off. Self-confidence, self-esteem, and a sense of security in a new environment are signs of bonding. There are roadblocks to bonding so caregivers must push the process of dealing with new converts and young disciples. There is no substitute for self-confidence and steadfastness.

SECTION TWO
(Conversion to 5 Months)

Character and Spiritual Development

The development process for converts depends on the convert's age and maturity at the time of conversion. First, the physical health of the convert must be determined. Then as part of the initial growth process, an honest assessment must be made as to the nature and level of spiritual understanding the conversion process and concept of discipleship. It is useful to know the family back-ground, level of education and the general knowledge base of the individual. All future spiritual growth is based on prior knowledge.

Should the level of moral character and spiritual development be limited, the mentor or coach will need to do remedial work along with surrogate care. It becomes obvious that the younger the convert is the easier it is to shore up the missing building blocks neglected in a past. It should be noted that when no positive steps were taken to develop these structures, the negative aspects of the environment did place some elements into the developmental mix.

Those who regularly care about young converts and the discipleship making process and the logical movement from bonding, to behavior, to knowledge base, to character and spiritual foundation have a difficult task. Some of these steps are age-specific or relevant to the maturity level and unless the substandard elements of their development are understood and corrected, a better quality of life may not be constructed. It took Saul of Tarsus (Paul) and Barnabas *"one whole year"* [365 days] working with converts in Antioch before they could be recognized as behaving in a Messiah-like manner which was later interpreted to be Christ-like.

Working with new converts and young believers is a long process and must never be undertaken in a hurried manner. After one year of effort supported by affection and prayer, an assessment shows major deficiencies, there is a deeper personal or spiritual problem that my need professional clergy or clinical attention. Although God is all powerful, there is no promise to take away the marks of sin on the physical body or the mind. When this point is reached, do not be reluctant to ask the pastoral staff or professionals for assistance. Never give up on the young, simply "turn them over" to others for additional advising and guidance.

One note of hope: when human efforts fail, there is divine intervention with authority and compassion to bring renewal, redemption, and restoration to the life of young believers. All humans stumble early in life. A stumble requires a quick step to keep from falling. When someone with whom you are working stumbles, act quickly; delay is difficult to overcome.

Negative conditioning was not the fault or choosing of the young; therefore, an informed and affectionate mentor or coach plus a loving and powerful God can make a real difference. Do not neglect to ask for divine assistance in this difficult process. God freely gives wisdom to those who ask in faith. Remember, God is not willing that any should perish but that all would come to the saving knowledge of the truth

Elements of Disposition and Temperament

Remedial development of the natural ability that affects behavior and the qualities of the mind and character are most important. The expression of individuality is recognizable soon after birth and grows for several years. A similar process happens in conversion, a change of behavior and expressions of moral character are obvious after conversion and continues to grow as the believer develops in grace. It is the totality of one's attitudes, interests, physical behavioral patterns, emotional responses, social roles, and other individual traits that endure over time. The building blocks of disposition and temperament are in place soon after conversion and develop as the believer grows in grace and knowledge. Some later events impact positive development of a mature disciple in the areas of mindset and lifestyle.

Residual traces of past abuse or an extended sinful lifestyle no longer control the disposition and lifestyle life. However, affection and patience, time and energy, and pleasant surroundings are required to move the maturing of discipleship forward. Bad stuff must be replaced with better elements to enable the person to cope with the realities of their present existence rather that dwelling on the negativity of the past. Additional effort in the arena of prayer and providence may do the rest – at least, all caregivers must do their best and leave the rest to a Higher Authority.

Some adults unknowingly lead the young astray through careless and inconsistent behavior. Certain behavior can influence the future action for several generations. It seems that patterns of immoral attitudes, behavior, and bad habits are passed to children and grandchildren from parents and grandparents (Exodus 20:5). Conversion is a crucial opportunity for rebuilding the foundation for life based on *"old things have passed away and all things have become new."*

Disposition is Complex

There are multiple factors that shape disposition and usually create a difference from others. It includes all of the patterns of thought and emotions that cause one to say and do things in a particular style. At a basic level, disposition is expressed through temperament, emotions and readily influences values, beliefs, and expectations. Research over several decades has pointed to hereditary factors, especially the basic emotional tone in the behavior. Yet, it is equally evident that the acquisition of values, beliefs, hope, and outlook are greatly influenced by early socialization and personal experiences. The gradual acceptance of the standard and practices of another culture influences personal development. Because of the process called enculturation, most individuals accept and adopt the traditions, rules, manners, and biases of the culture in which they develop and grow. This fact gives caregivers a role in personal development of the new folk who enter their group. Always do things in moderation and cultivate hope in the future.

Many scholars agree that (1) disposition and (2) environment are influential in the development of human character. Disposition may depend on genetic factors and is often called *nature*, while the environment is called *nurture*. It is clear that both nature and nurture are factors in convert development into growing disciples.

USE SPACE FOR NOTES

SECTION THREE
(conversion to 6 months)

Crisis in Personal Development

Erik Erikson provided an early description (1956) of development in the young. According to Erikson, the socialization process of an individual consists of eight steps, each one accompanied by an emotional and a social crisis that must be resolved for the individual to adequately handle the next stage of development. These phases also impact spiritual development, with five occurring during early life: infancy, childhood, and adolescence--a time period most relevant to the conversion process and discipleship growth and development.

Stage One:

When the young are well-nurtured and loved during the first two years of life, they develop hope by learning basic trust. When these first two years are influenced by bad nurturing and a negative environment, the infant becomes insecure and learns to mistrust which is the opposite of hope. To have hope one must develop two things: desire and expectancy. When children desire and expect a good response from others they develop hope, when they are disappointed they develop mistrust.

Stage Two:

The second stage begins in about two years and lasts until for another two years.

The early part of this stage may include stubbornness, and negativism depending on the individual's disposition. This early phase may influence negative nurturing response and thus influence future growth. This stage is when autonomy (self-sufficiency and independence) is developed or a sense of (shame, discomfort, humiliation, or embarrassment). This is when the "human will" is developed that produces willpower, resolve, or spirit which provides essential enthusiasm for life. A well cared for person emerges from this phase with self-confidence, and happy with their newly found control. However, negative nurturing behavior during the early stage can greatly harm positive development.

Stage Three:

The early part of the third stage is considered the "play, stay and education phase," when the young develops a sense of purpose and goes through a learning initiative or guilt period where they learn the words fault, blame, and experiences the feeling of remorse or sorrow. They learn broader skills through cooperation. And learn to work with others, and to lead as well as follow. If this phase is not adequately negotiated, the young may depend excessively on others and never develop leadership skills needed in the family and faith-based group.

Stage Four:

This stage has to do with basic competence skills in learning essential elements of their education. They learn to master more formal and spiritual skills that facilitate their learning foundational truths and basic academic skills that assist their natural development and their spiritual development. Any faith-based or spiritual formation will not come from the academic system; yet the foundation gained there will assist in learning sacred literature which must be supplied by family and faith-based groups. During this phase the need for self-discipline grows each year. Those who adequately negotiated the earlier stages will become trusting, filled with initiative, autonomous, and industrious.

Stage Five:

This fifth stage relates to learning identity where the young are pushed in various directions. As maturity develops the young are pulled and pushed child in many directions. The well-adjusted child avoids delinquency and looks toward achievement. Later in the period, a clear sexual identity is established as to why and for what purpose God intended a gender difference. Caregivers begin to inspire, and gradually ideals to live by are formulated. Assisting the young, a new convert, or a new disciple through the various stages of emotional development is a complex and difficult task. However, the end is worth the journey.

Although scholars do not always agree on the process of development, they normally agree that there are critical periods in development where the young will be more sensitive to guidance. Most agree that developmental needs should be met in a family-type environment or in a wholesome faith-based atmosphere that attempts to maintain a family-type sense of belonging.

Culture becomes an important environmental factor. Europe and the United States of America have maintained individualistic cultures and emphasized individual needs. In contrast, Asia, Africa, Central and South America are characterized by community-centric cultures that focus on belonging to a larger group, such as family or nation. In such cultures, cooperation is more important than competitiveness, and this necessarily affects moral and spiritual development.

SECTION FOUR
(Conversion to Nine Months)

Steps in Character Building

Character is the set of affective, cognitive, and behavioral patterns gleaned from personal life experience that determines how one thinks, feels, and behaves. Character continues to develop throughout life, although much depends on inborn traits and early life experiences. Character is also related to the level of moral development. While the debate continues as to which of these provide the most influence, most scholars agree that good watch care is critical to the development of character. Caregivers who have the facts can adapt surrogate nurturing to the disposition and environment and provide guidance and influence the development of good character and a mature

USE SPACE FOR NOTES

attitude toward the world. Positive spiritual formation is a result of good character development.

USE SPACE FOR NOTES

SECTION FIVE
(Conversion to 11 Months)

Spiritual Formation

    Just as all the other steps in development, spiritual formation begins before birth and continues through about age eleven. Spiritual formation is influenced by significant events in life, personal experiences, parental and adult behavior, observation of peers, and social changes in or near their early environment. Much is done to assist development but in many respects parents and caregivers miss the core needs: personal spirituality.

Spirituality in the Young

    Normally the young were thought to be too self-centered to process supernatural abstracts or theoretical concepts. Scholars believed the young just absorbed values and beliefs from others. More recently research has demonstrated that even the very young are interested in both the supernatural and the nature of being, and this includes right and wrong, good and evil, life and death, and the existence of God. The young want their world to have meaning.

It is important to note that spiritual formation is not all positive; it depends on the person or persons providing the information and the context in which the concept and constructs related to spirituality are presented. Spiritual formation is a central aspect of development and takes place both negatively and positively regardless of age, faith-based connections, basic beliefs, family values, or worldview. Spirituality is not age-specific; it relates more to maturity and knowledge than to age. The young seem to have an inner clock and compass which guides their life, but at times they must be instructed to observe and follow those inner impulses.

When the young ask, "Would it be wrong for me to do….?" It is a good sign that the inner soul light is burning. A wise proverb (Proverbs 20:27) states, "*The spirit of man is the candle of the Lord searching all the inner parts…*" Everyone, has a conscience that searches out the inner bad stuff. This inner spirit leads in the direction of the good path unless older people teach bad habits by example and enable others to make poor choices. At times the word spiritual is too comprehensive a concept for the young to grasp, so one speaks of being good, obeying the rules, listening to mature friends, not taking things that do not belong to you, or telling things that are not true. These steps build character and the elements of character are the basic building blocks of spiritual formation.

Perhaps one would not find their way through this world without some aspects of spiritual formation. The secular folk may want to call it moral character, but that is where good things start. A person of good character is just a small step from becoming spiritual. The pieces of spiritual formation slip into life at the early stages of development often without the individual's knowledge. At times the adults involved in caring for the young do not see verbal indications that the idea or concept has taken hold, but the seeds are planted. Train up a child in the way they should go and when they are old they will remember.

The Greek version of "spiritual" was illustrated by what they called awareness. The Greeks had three aspects of personal awareness: 1) awareness of self, 2) awareness of self in the world, and 3) awareness of a higher power. When a person realized the value of self and understood that the higher power had placed them in the world for a purpose, and that the world was made by this same higher power, the emotion was felt in what the Greeks called the "heart." These steps may be similar to spiritual awareness and are the first steps to spiritual formation.

Consider the steps more closely. First, self-awareness or self-worth and self-esteem are the essential ingredients of spirituality. Second, an awareness of the awesome world in which one exists and moves in time and space. Third, awareness that a higher power has placed one in this world for a purpose: the emotion felt in the heart when all this awareness comes together is the fountain-head of spirituality.

Most everyone has their own way of feeling spiritual and others must never impose their version of private or faith-based religiosity on the young. Personal spirituality is much like "hash in grandma's kitchen," it accumulates over time and grandma mixes a little love and seasoning with the hash to make it good to the taste and nutritious and serves it hot with love.

This is the nearest explanation available to explain spirituality in the lives of the young. A care giver should only answer the questions that the Spirit prompts the young to ask. Spiritual things must accumulate and should be kindled by the Holy Spirit and warmed by the affection of a mature and loving caregiver.

Some tend to identify spirituality with having made an intentional choice to accept an offer of salvation, be baptized, attend worship, read the Bible, etc. Developing a spiritual nature is much more than an event or a decision; it is an ongoing lifestyle and becomes a part of the fabric of one's being and the essence of who one really has become. Being spiritual is not following or obeying rules; it is having a change of heart that causes one to want to obey and follow the right path through all aspects of life. This provides one with purpose and direction for life.

With emerging research to convince faith-based caregivers that giving attention to spirituality really matters, it still takes courage in a secular society to adopt spirituality as a natural dimension of development. This is distinct from sectarian religion or practicing the faith of a particular denomination; it has to do with full personal development in the area of morality, ethics, and faith-based living. The goal of nurturing is to establish sound ethical foundations for living that matures into a missional lifestyle.

Caregivers and Spiritual Formation

Caregivers should never talk directly about spirituality, instead they should watch for an opportunity to cultivate natural interest in honesty, fairness, morality, ethics, and justice. Custodial personnel should articulate their own spiritual autobiography or journey and share it with others. The vocabulary used and any diversity between behavior and personal experience would become obvious. Identify common difficulties such as death of a love one, loss of job, or other experiences that impact the way one thinks about God and justice. Do not seek consensus, but wrestle with the relationship between religion and spirituality and understanding the difference.

USE SPACE FOR NOTES

SECTION SIX
(After the first year following Conversion)

Monitor Adverse Peer Influence

Among the most destructive things that can happen to New converts is to become socially involved with peers who have bad habits, immoral behavior and weak character. In the general population it is difficult to restrict all such associations because the restriction has the reverse effect. This means that the associates of converts and young disciples should be monitored, and each negative incident promptly dealt with by a loving friend. Constructive talk is crucial at this point.

Over a period of months, individuals in a particular group tend to become more similar in behavior to others in the same group. Most want to belong to a popular group and the peer pressure from the group to conform, accounts for the influence of such groups. Caregivers must provide constructive guidance to peer associations.

USE SPACE FOR NOTES

SECTION SEVEN
(First 6 Months of the Second Year)

Adult Role Models

Adult role models such as teachers, parents of peers, etc. begin to have significant influence. What faith-based groups and custodial care plans to do to prepare the young or the real world must be done before the late teens or a new and special efforts must be established to deal with changes in adolescent behavior.

USE SPACE FOR NOTES

SECTION EIGHT
(The 6 months prior to the second anniversary of conversion)

Stop the World, I Want to get off!

By the time young people near the end of their teens, they have learned the cost of going to school, driving a car, or living on their own. They often return to parents or grandparents for assistance with school or living expenses. This should not be discouraged. It gives the family a "second chance" to influence their future. At this point they are usually open to mature guidance about life and living. The world can be a scary place and unless they have a family or spiritual anchor, they will turn to artificial support that leads to becoming involved with the wrong people. Any negativity passed to a young person at this stage most likely will be counter-productive. Be positive. Philosophy taught that one could never reach a positive conclusion beginning with a negative premise; yet, a positive declaration always implies a negative situation. The old proverb *"accentuate the positive and eliminate the negative"* should be observed.

Kingdom Growth Through Missional Behavior

—Growing a Relational Congregation

Afterword

This is a delightful and fascinating book, which will possibly contain the most useful material that an ambitious and mission fixated church could ever study. That Hollis Green has done a remarkable job in memorializing in written form his vast amount of experience, ecclesiastical, missional and theological, will immediately become obvious to the reader, whose ministry will be benefited in a plethora of lambent different ways.

In this work, the reader will be exposed to a treasury of thoughts, both intellectual and affective, demonstrating the distillation of many years of experience in actualizing the Kingdom of God. Dr. Green has reduced the aims and aspirations of the overcoming pastor to what is almost a logical and scientific methodology, augmented and secured by God's Spirit. All the possible dimensions of Church Growth are examined and evaluated with experiential, Biblically based accuracy and psychological insights. The essence of *koionia* is recognized and the methodology proposed is founded on education and proper exegesis of God's Word.

The emphasis on the similarities of the growth of a local Christian Assembly to human reproductive physiology is unique. The various stages of human growth and development from the neonatal to the adolescent to adulthood are shown to be very similar to the growth stages in a local congregation.

This recount of practical experience, psychological and theological wisdom is here made available to the neophyte and to the experienced worker in God's vineyard in a way that will be easy and useful to follow.

E. Basil Jackson, MD, ThD, PhD, DSc, DLitt

About the Authors

Hollis L. Green, ThD, PhD, DLitt, is a Clergy-Educator with public relations and business credentials and doctorates in theology, philosophy, and education. A Distinguished Professor of Education and Social Change at the graduate level for over

four decades, Dr. Green is a Diplomate in the Oxford Society of Scholars, and author of 50+ books and numerous articles. He served six years as a member of the U.S. Senate Business Advisory Board and with certified membership in several public relations societies (RPRC, PRSA, and IPRC). He served pastorates in five states, a Military Chaplain during the Vietnam era, a denominational official for 18 years, and traveled in ministry and lectured in over 100 countries.

Dr. Green was the founder (1974) of Associated Institutional Developers (AID) Ltd., an international Public Relations and Corporate Consultant Company. He was Vice-President (1974-1979) of Luther Rice Seminary (www.lru.edu) and became the founding President (1981) and Chancellor (1991-2008) of Oxford Graduate School, [www.ogs.edu]. As part of a global outreach, Dr. Green founded OASIS UNIVERSITY (2002) in Trinidad, W. I. [www.oasisgradedu.org] where continues to serve as Chancellor. In 2004, he assisted in establishing

Greenleaf Global Educational Foundation in Colorado to advance issues related to the current needs of education.

In addition to his other endeavors, Dr. Green launched Global Educational Advance, Inc. (2007) [www.gea-books.com] to advance higher education and social change through publishing, curriculum development, library/ learning resources, instruction, and global book distribution with 30,000 distributors in 100 countries to advance social change. His books and assisting authors in publishing are a logical outgrowth of a sixty-year ministry through education. He serves the Author-Publisher Partnership PRESS as Corporate Chair and Co-publisher with his sons, Barton and Brian. Dr. Green continues to travel, speak, teach, write books and work with authors in publishing as his health permits.

ABOUT THE AUTHORS

E. Basil Jackson, MD, ThD, PhD, DSc, DLitt, is a Distinguished Professor of Psychiatry, Medicine and Law. He was born and raised in Ireland and received his preliminary education there. Dr. Jackson is a respected academic with multiple doctorates from major universities. As such, he has made significant

impact in the field of integration of religion and society. A well-traveled man, skilled in several languages, Jackson has ministered to both the physical and spiritual needs of needy people around the globe.

Dr. Jackson studied at the Queen's University of Belfast Medical School and shortly after graduation was appointed to a fellowship in psychiatry at the Menninger School of Psychiatry in Topeka, Kansas. After completion of training in Adult Psychiatry he entered the child psychiatry program at the University of Rochester in Rochester, New York. Shortly after completing training as a pediatric psychiatrist, he was appointed Director of Graduate Psychiatric Education at Marquette University School of Medicine in Milwaukee, Wisconsin.

Jackson has been certified in Psychiatry, Child Psychiatry and Forensic Psychiatry and completed training and certification as a psychoanalyst and also as an addictionologist. He has practiced these disciplines all of his professional life. Dr. Jackson has also earned graduate degrees in theology and in law and is a member of the Bar of the State of Wisconsin. Presently he continues to consult in the field of law and psychiatry, but his principal interest lies in the integration of faith and society. He has authored a number of books; four recent additions to Dr. Jackson's list of scholarly writings are:

- *Cherished Gemstones From History*
- *Competency To Stand Trial*
- *The Faith Dynamic: A Treatise on Creationism and Evolutionary Theory*
- *A Psycho-Theological Exploration of New Testament Concepts*

Appendix A

OTHER BOOKS BY Hollis L. Green

To understand the problems that small Faith-based entities have gaining and retaining new constituencies, extensive research was done during the past two decades. Meanwhile, my schedule was filled with academic administration, teaching, research and writing, but colleagues and friends have encouraged sequels to my best-known works. My last twenty (20+) books were an attempt to follow that prompt.

- *Why Churches Die*. *(2007)* **ISBN 978-1-9796019-03** A fresh assessment of congregational vitality to determine thirty-five reasons why faith-based congregations were losing their pristine power of outreach.

- *Interpreting an Author's Words*. *(2008)* **ISBN 978-0980-164-74**—Define both formal and informal study and writing skills by understanding how to clearly interpret the spoken and written words of others.

- *Sympathetic Leadership Cybernetics*. *(2010)* **ISBN 978-1-9354345-28** – This work attempts to clarify management and leadership in the context of organizational and institutional functionality and charts a course for organizations to serve the needs of people through shepherd management and servant leadership.

- *Why Christianity Fails in America.* *(2010)* **ISBN 978-0-9796019-10**-- A call for an internal redirection of the heart and soul to make the pristine faith viable in the Twenty-first century.

- *How to Build a Better Spouse Trap. (2010)* **ISBN 978-1—9354344-50** – A major failure of faith-based groups is they have made little difference in the lives of individuals and their function in the family. How to choose a mate, learn for our mistakes, stay married, and teach others to break the cycle of dysfunctional relationships. The family unit is a microcosm of faith-based behavior.

- *Discipleship. (2010)* **ISBN 978-0-9796019-5-8**-- A revived edition to better explain the process of a believer's lifestyle from conversion (change direction), to discipleship (learning), to apostle (mature enough to be trusted with the message of grace.)

- *SO TALES. (2011)* **ISBN 978-1-9354345-80** -- Preserving true 240 true stories from the past for the benefit of family and friends.

- *Designing Valid Research. (2011)* **ISBN 978-1-9354345-73** – A guide to designing a research proposal and developing a social scientific dissertation.

- *Titanic Lessons. (2012)* **ISBN 978-0-9796019-6-5** – An effort to demonstrate that bigger is not necessarily better and that all building of machines, organizations, and institutions must use material that meets the precise requirements of the task. This must be applied to people, process, and functionality of the human element and the mechanics must match the environment.

- *Why Wait Till Sunday?* (2012) **ISBN 978-1-935434-27-6**-- A renewal plan for older congregations who depended on programs coming down from sectarian authority rather than locally generated ideas and involvement in seven (7) aspects of renewal.

- *Fighting the Amalekites. (2013)* **ISBN 978-1-935434-30-6** – The unhealthy addictions, unproductive habits, an uncontrolled tongue are all little "Amalekites" unless these are destroyed they will become the destroyer. These join the Amalekites that ambush and take advantage of spiritual weaknesses.

- *Remedial and Surrogate Parenting (2013)* **ISBN 978-1-9354344-81** --Children are a gift of God and a legacy of faith-based families; therefore, nurturing skills are an essential aspect of religion. This work is guidance for remedial human development (0-20) for parents, teachers, and childcare workers.

- *The EVERGREEN Devotional New Testament – C.A.F.E. Edition. (2015, 2018)* **ISBN 978-1-9354342-69** – *EDNT is a* 42-year project to translate common NT Greek and determine the meaning "then" and how words can best be expressed "now" and remain true to the original intent expressed in a common devotional language.

- *Transformational Leadership in Education: Second Edition (2013)* **ISBN 978-1-935434-23-8** -- *A* strengths-based approach to education for administrators, teachers, and guidance counselors.

- *Tear Down These Walls*. (2013) **ISBN 978-1-9354341-84** -- A priority agenda must be to make people moral citizens of the world before they can become mystical citizens of heaven. Where organized groups choose not to function, personal action could make a difference and break down some of the barriers that divide the faith-based community and strengthen the "One Lord-One Faith–One Baptism" message.

- *Recycled Words n' Stuff. (2016)* **ISBN 978-1-935434-86-3** – A collection of short narratives and essays of general interest.

- *The Children's Bread: Accessing Faith-Based Economics and Personal Wealth By Unlocking Whole Life Stewardship* (2018)

  ISBN 978-1-935434-90-0– ppreciating faith-based economics and personal wealth to unlock a missional lifestyle and funding for humanitarian and faith-based entities.

- *Kingdom Growth through Missional Behavior (2019)* **ISBN 97 8-1-935434-91-7** -- adopting the thinking, behaviors, and practices of a missionary in order to globalize the message of grace

Books in Process

- **Beyond Pulpit, Classroom, and Lectern (**2020a)— Unlocking exposition and Instruction in Subject Matter Sharing. . **ISBN 978-1-950839-03-2**

- **God Has Confidence in You!"** (2020b) –"…they lived in caves and holes in the   earth and obtained a good report through faith" **ISBN 978-1-950839-04-9**

- **Research Methods for Problem Solvers and Critical Thinkers.** *(2019b)* **ISBN 978-1-950839-00-1** --Guidance in developing a master's thesis, designing a doctoral research proposal and constructing a defendable dissertation based on social scientific research with an objective of positive social change.

- **All Believers are Converted Equal** (2021a) – *Unlocking the Path to Moral Excellence. (Based on 2 Peter Chapter One.*
- **Contextualization and Positive Social Change** (2021b) –*Strategies for Integrating Moral Values Families, Communities, Faith-based Entities and Society*
- ***A Strategy for Positive Social Change*** *(2021c) –reclaiming the moral high ground in society by developing commonalities in a multi-cultural society.*

■ **PLUS THESE 12 CHILDREN'S BOOKS:** In keeping with the Dons of Oxford University, a dozen Children's Novellas available on PDF or E-books:

- ■ • Sleepy Town Lullaby and Story;
- ■ • The Funky Chicken's Wedding;
- ■ • The Scoop about Birthday Soup;
- ■ • Cranky Not-so-Hottra'
- ■ • Cat-Astropic Charlie;
- ■ • A Tea Party at Nany's House;
- ■ • The Shimonaka Big Dripper;
- ■ • The Mouse of the House;
- ■ • The Boy Who Wanted to Grow a Beard;
- ■ • The Trouble with Funny Book Cussing;
- ■ • The Blue Jay and Grandma's Song;
- ■ • Ditala Killed a Dead Snake

Global Ed Advance, PRESS -- Printed in Australia, Brazil, Canada, China, Germany, India, Italy, Poland, Russia, South Korea, Spain, UK, and USA, and available on the Espresso Book Machine© or any place good books are sold. Order books from www.gea-books.com/bookstore/

Appendix B

Compare Your Church with the Seven Churches
STRENGTHS AND WEAKNESSES WORKSHEET

Commendations for *Strength and Virtues*	Rebuked for *Sins and Weaknesses*

3. SARDIS – (Good reputation but about to Die)

-2. PERGAMOS – (Good people influenced by an evil pace)

-1. LAODICEA – (Lukewarm and living in spiritual poverty)

0. EPHESUS – (Orthodoxy without love)

+1. THYATIRA – (Active but weakened by Immorality)

+2. SMYRNA – (Suffering poverty but spiritually rich)

+3. PHILADELPHIA – (Faithful but too weak to Grow)

Compare Your Church with Each Below:

Weak   **Circle the Number**   Strong

0____1____2____3____4____5____6____7____8____9____10____

SARDIS – (Good reputation but about to die)
Weak   Strong

0____1____2____3____4____5____6____7____8____9____10____

PERGAMOS – (Good people influenced by an evil place)
Weak   Strong

0____1____2____3____4____5____6____7____8____9____10____

LAODICEA – (Lukewarm and living in spiritual poverty)
Weak   Strong

0____1____2____3____4____5____6____7____8____9____10____

THYATIRA – (Active but weakened by Immorality)
Weak   Strong

0____1____2____3____4____5____6____7____8____9____10____

SMYRNA – (Suffering poverty but spiritually rich)
Weak   Strong

0____1____2____3____4____5____6____7____8____9____10____

PHILADELPHIA – (Faithful but too weak to grow)

Weak   Strong

0____1____2____3____4____5____6____7____8____9____10____

EPHESUS – (Orthodoxy without love)

Weak   Strong

0____1____2____3____4____5____6____7____8____9____10____

Add the circled numbers [   ] to determine weak or strong:

Highest is 70

[0 – 35 WEAK; 42 - 70 STRONG.]

Appendix C

Academy Primary and Secondary Age-level Divisions

(Each age-level division has a lead teacher and one assistant or aide.) The Academy may be phased in: Primary divisions then Secondary.

Primary Academic Age-Level Divisions

- **Primary Division One**

    K-Primary 1: age range 4 - 6.

    1-Primary 2: age range 5 - 7.

- **Primary Division Two**

    2-Primary 3: age range 6 - 8.

    3-Primary 4: age range 7 - 9.

- **Primary Division Three**

    4-Primary 5: age range 8 - 10.

    5-Primary 6: age range 9 - 11.

    6-Primary 7: age range 10 - 12.

Secondary Academic Age-Level Division

- **First-third Secondary Division**

    7-First year: age range 11 - 13.

    8-Second year: age range 12 - 14.

Middle-third Secondary Division

9-Third year: age range 13 - 15.

10-Fourth year: age range 14 - 16.

Upper-third Secondary Division

11-Fifth year: age range 15 - 17.
(*AS-level* = **A**dvanced **S**tudy

12-Sixth year: age range 16 - 18.
(*AS2- level* = Higher education placement)

Standard Tests available for USA or specific Countries on request from <u>GlobalEdAdvance@aol.com</u>

Appendix D

Guidance for Caregivers, Mentors, and Coaches

When faith-based entities fail to reach a community with the message of social ethics and morality, children and families become dysfunctional. Practitioners and professionals may succeed with basic assistance that produce social services, but this is a stop gap measure. Individuals are limited in what they can do to solve the systemic problem of abandoned, neglected and abused individuals. In addition to community leaders, members of the social professions are confronted daily with the dysfunctional fallout of broken families, broken laws, and broken promises. Yet community leaders and the social professions have an opportunity for a contextual understanding of the secular market place often lost to faith-based leaders. In the past, an application of the essential elements of morality and fairness was left to clergy, academics, judiciary, and law enforcement who have limited contact and little understanding of the realities of the complex community and the dysfunctional families that produce most of the problems of society. There remains a great fixed gulf between the moral convictions and the constructive community agenda. Sadly, the core values and moral fiber of the community have diminished and created a contextual atmosphere that breeds discrimination, segregation and a lack of justice or fairness for all concerned.

Why does morality and ethics have difficulty in a multicultural society? Why are children the primary victims of broken promises, broken laws, and broken families? What is the inferior process that weakens the moral fiber? Why has the faith-based message of grace and forgiveness failed to be a viable expression of morality to the community? To integrate basic moral values into a pluralistic community, individuals and groups must have a comprehensive grasp of the many aspects of culture and tradition and face them with an open mind and a willing heart. Priority must be given to the welfare of the children; then the community can begin to fix the problems that produced the problems. Hopefully, faith-based groups will have a productive role in this cure and care of souls.

Why has caring for the young failed? Parents are to dwell together in harmony, so their prayers would not be hindered. Partners in marriage are obligated to separate each other from participation in the immorality of the community lest their children become defiled. Yet, all individuals are responsible to a higher authority to conduct their lives in keeping with moral and ethical standards. When these standards are broken everyone suffers, but the young and undereducated endure the most hardships and long-term difficulties. This is the arena where faith-based entities and moral citizens must function to bring the young into harmony with divine intentions. There seems to be a mixing bowl of culture and tradition

Catalyst or Change Agent

A failure to understand the basic difference in children is much the same as confusing a catalyst and a change agent. Both have the same objective – producing change, but one is not changed in the process. There can be no true change in the children unless those precipitating the change are also changed as part of the ongoing progression. It must be an interactive process. Any failure to understand the difference between a catalyst and a functioning change agent has frustrated child caregivers for decades. A catalyst is not changed in the process of creating the course of action that brings about change in a child; a change agent is altered by the course of action itself and becomes a different functioning element. When caregivers begin to alter and change their attitude and behavior, the child will more readily see the need to make changes. It is this reciprocal or mutually responsive process that makes care giving work.

Surrogate Caregivers Concerns

All caregivers and surrogate nurturers must be concerned with the assessed levels of bonding, personality, knowledge base, character, and spiritual formations as they deal with the children. As new children come into a custodial facility, or new converts inter a place of worship, there is a time lag in adjusting to the new environment. Everyone must be sensitive to this observable occurrence.

One may appropriately translate the early months of life in which they develop a relationship with authority. During the next 6 months the child develops a sense of expectation from the environment. At about one year, the child begins to develop the beginnings of autonomy: walking, talking freely and thinking positively about the environment. This growth and development process continues, and the progress should be recognized. As a child reaches early age and goes outside the facility for class, it takes about 6 months to learn the rules and develop relationships with new teachers. This is called socialization. During the next 6 months the child develops a sense of empathy in relationship with peers, adults, and teachers and is taught the meaning of justice and the expectations of their surroundings.

Most of problems of behavior could be corrected at this stage if caregivers and teachers operated through tough love to adjust attitudes and actions. Much of the funds spent on the courts and prisons could be diverted to improving the conditions for the children. When the teen years are entered, it is much harder to make the necessary adjustments and/or corrections.

Confidence is a Factor

Remedial development and growth begin with confidence. There must be confidence in the watch care provided, confidence in the program and process being utilized as a priority, and also have confidence in the personnel and staff with whom one works. Without confidence in these areas, no individual care facility or program can function effectively regardless of the quality or quantity of personnel and funding.

These factors must be considered in the remedial and surrogate nurturing of converts and young disciples. Understanding how different individuals function in the context of the basic institutions is important to growth and development. Age, background and experience have dissimilar impact on different individuals. All converts and new members of a faith-based group are not equal and must be considered as individuals with both age-level maturity, background, positive and negative experience and personal and emotional feelings. To ignore these aspects is to fail as a nurturing caregiver.

Nurturing is Situational

What may be good care for one person at a particular stage of development may not be good care for another or even for the same person at a different developmental stage. Good care does two things: it matches the person's stage of development, and it empowers the individual to progress toward self-direction. Good care is situational, yet it provides the long-term development. The entire nurturing system is based on a growth and development from high structure to little or no structure, from a kindergarten-type beginning to work in which the structure or task is lessened over time and the relationship between mentor/coach and the convert or new member becomes less until the individual is able to function on their own in the real world.

Quality and Quantity

Quality and quantity are mutually exclusive; increase one and decrease the other. There must be a proportional balance between these two elements to maintain stable growth and development. There is a limit to what one person can do for another in the spiritual realm. If the staff is short-handed or unskilled, all the new folk undergo some unpleasantness and suffer personal loss. Perfection is not the goal of spiritual care; growth and age-specific development is the true objective. Quality in spiritual watch care comes when new converts and new members have a guide, coach, counselor, and friend who provide the freedom to search and learn and discover the way forward. Discovery is real learning and should be rewarded with marks of quality and words of praise.

Critical Path Method (CPM)

The Critical Path Method works backward from a perception of where the person should be at the mature stage. CPM is used in construction when a builder views both an architect drawing of a completed building and a set of working drawings of how the building is to be constructed. The builder, with a clear view of both plans and a conception of the finished product, establishes target dates for each stage of development. The objective is to prepare an individual for the real world when they reach spiritual maturity.

Working back from the target date, the builder considers time, material, and contingencies to establish a construction schedule. At this point the builder must start at the beginning, structure the building in stages, and arrange for an evaluation process based on the architect's plans. Each aspect of the construction must be done in sequence with the timeline affected by the duration of each stage. With the CPM the builder may evaluate progress using a Performance Evaluation Review Technique (PERT). To do this, the mentor/coach must understand clearly the age-specific level of development of each person. Age or physical size is not sufficient criteria to judge progress because each individual is different.

Conversion is to turn in a different direction and be transformed; to be *converted* is turning outward to be visible. Some call the process of a new birth as being converted to the Lord. This is a positive process of turning from an old life and moving in the direction of a new lifestyle. The opposite of this is expressed in the Story of the Prodical Son: the wasteful son converted his inheritance from property and "stuff" to something visible (cash). *And after a few days, the younger son converted all to cash and took his journey to a far country, and there he squandered his inheritance in wasteful living. (*Luke 15:13 EDNT)

Should there be an *Office of Spiritual Birthing*? When Bible translators took the concept of Elders and made the Office of Bishop and Deacon, perhaps they should have added an Office of Spiritual Birthing. The old English "midwife" meant *with woman; yes, a male who assists with a birth is also a "midwife."* What about conversion; as a new birth do we not need some special workers who function as a spiritual birthing agent? Of course, we have to come up with a better name than *midwife*! What about: believers who are loving mothers and wise fathers. *The fruit of the righteous is a tree of life; and he that wins souls is wise.* (Proverb 11:30)

> *What does the word that we preach say? It is near you, even in your mouth, and in your heart; 9. if you acknowledge with your mouth the message that Jesus is Lord, and believe in your heart that God stood Him up from the grave, you shall be saved. 10. For with the heart man believes and is justified; and with the mouth he confirms his salvation. 11. The scripture declares that whoever believes on Him shall not be disappointed. (Romans 10:8-11 EDNT)*

> *37. Although Jesus did many miracles in their presence, they did not believe in Him: 38. So the words of Prophet Isaiah might be fulfilled, Lord, who has believed our report? And to whom has the arm of the Lord been revealed? 39.*

> *The reason they could not believe, is recorded in Isaiah, 40. He has blinded their eyes, and hardened their heart; that they should not see with their eyes, nor understand with their heart, and be converted, and I should heal them. 41. Isaiah said these things, about Jesus when he saw His glory, and spoke of Him. 42. Nevertheless, many of the chief rulers believed on Him; but because of the Pharisees they did not confess Him, lest they should be put out of the synagogue: 43. They preferred the approval of men, more than the approval of God. (John 12:37-43 EDNT)*

Provided one follows the path of Jesus from the manger to the Cross, they will see a footpath of self-denial, exhausting travel, and daily service to those in need. Luke wrote, *"Jesus healed all in need of healing."* Loving service to others was His food and drink and the will of the Father that nourished His earthly life. Consequently, those who follow Jesus will live a sacrificial life demonstrating care and concern for others.

Jesus chose to endow His followers with blessings to share with others. There is no room for selfishness or laziness in the life of those who take up their cross and follow the footpath of discipleship. Those who walk in the spirit of Jesus will live a clean life, be part of a wholesome family, and regularly participate in outreach and kingdom support. Giving of self and personal resources are part of the blessing. Jesus said, *"It is more blessed to give than receive."* Why, because one who gives has more than enough and is blessed to share the overage with others. The needy are blessed, but those who supply the material resources to assist the needy are doubly blessed. As my friend, Subesh said, *"They gather blessings to scatter to others."* This is kingdom growth through a missional lifestyle.

Not only will committed believers share their God-given resources, they will become personally involved in the work. It is a hands-on lifestyle for them and their family. The harvest fields are ripe and ready for gathering, but not enough labors to complete the task. In 2 Kings 19:3 Hezekiah sent a proverbial message to Isaiah about the divided kingdoms of Israel and Judah being too weak to resist captivity: *"We are like a poor traveling women about to collapse without strength to bring their children to birth."* This is similar to the circumstance of the modern-day church. Souls ready for the kingdom, but there is no strength to complete the birthing process. Individuals, families, places of worship, countries and nations seem to be a similar place of weakness as far as advancing the kingdom of God.

> *1. As we work together with God, we appeal to you not to accept. the grace of God and let it go to waste. 2. God said, I have heard your prayers at a convenient time, and in the day of salvation I have brought you relief in a difficult situation: observe, now is the time for coming together; now is the day of deliverance. (2 Corinthians 6:1-2 EDNT)*

> *1. So, then, let us leave elementary teaching about Christ behind us and pass on to full growth; no need to lay the foundations all over again, the change of heart which turns away from lifeless observations, the faith which*

*turns towards God, 2. of the instructions about different kinds of baptisms, about the laying on of hands, and of resurrection from the dead, and upon that sentence that lasts all of eternity. 3. God willing, this is our plan. 4. It is impossible to renew to repentance those who were enlightened, those who tasted the free gift from heaven, and those who were partakers of the Holy Spirit. 5. And have tasted the goodness of the word of God, and felt the powers of the world to come, 6. if they fall away, they cannot attain repentance, seeing they crucify the Son of God a second time, and are exposing Him to public contempt. 7. For when the earth drinks in the rain that comes often upon it and when it brings forth herbage useful to those who work the ground. It receives a share of the blessing from God; 8. but if the earth produces thorns and thistles it has lost its value; a curse hangs over it, and it will feed the bonfire. 9. **But we are confident of better things of you, beloved, things that go together with salvation. 10. God is not an unjust God that he should forget all you have done as a labor of love that you displayed in that you have been and still are active in the service of God's dedicated people.** 11. But our great longing is to see you all showing the same eagerness right up to the end: 12. so that you do not become lethargic, but imitate those who through faith and patience inherit the promises. (Hebrews 6:1-12 EDNT)*

11. The story laid upon me is long and hard to explain, seeing you are so dull of hearing. 12. After all this time you should be teachers, yet you still need to be taught again the first principles of the divine revelation: you have gone back to needing milk instead of solid food. 13. Those who still have milk for their diet do not have the experience to speak of what is right: remains an infant. 14. But grown men can eat solid food, those who, through the development of the right kind of habit, have reached a stage when their perceptions are trained to distinguish between good and evil. 7. You were running the race well; who cut in to obstruct your obedience of the truth? 8. This readiness to believe without evidence does not come from the one who called you. 9. It is true that a little yeast can change the whole batch of dough. 10. I am persuaded in the Lord to have confidence in you, that you will not be led astray: but whoever is shaking your faith will pay the penalty at judgment. 11. And brethren, if I preach circumcision, why do I still suffer persecution? Then the offence which the cross causes would cease. 12. I wish they who upset your mind would make eunuchs of themselves. (Galatians 5:7-12 EDNT)

Appendix E

Guidance for New Converts

First Things First

2. since you are newly born, yearn for the unadulterated milk of the word, so you may grow up until your soul thrives in good health. 3. Since you have tasked (tasted) the Lord's kindness. 4. Draw near to him; He is the living fulfillment of the stone discarded by men but chosen of God. 5. **You yourselves are lively stones built into a spiritual house; you must be a holy priesthood to offer up spiritual sacrifices acceptable to God by Jesus Christ.** (*1 Peter 2:2-5 EDNT*)

Soul-Winners are Important to Converts

14. I write this not to your shame, but as my beloved children, I warn you. 15. For though you have ten thousand tutors in Christ, you have only one father in Christ Jesus, I have begotten you through the gospel. 16. Wherefore, I beseech you, follow my footsteps. (*1 Corinthians 4:14-16 EDNT*)

Good and Bad Behavior

*19. Now t***he behavior that belongs to the flesh is obvious***, they are: (**sensual sins**) unfaithfulness in marriage, unrestrained living, unbridled acts of indecency; 20. (**religious sins**) the worship of idols, the use of drugs and* *magical powers; (**temperamental sins**) hostility, strife, jealousy, violent flare-ups of temper, self-seeking ambitions, adherence to contradictory teaching; 21. (**personal sins**) desires to appropriate what others have, drunkenness and carousing, and similar things: I warned you before that people who do such things will have no part in the kingdom of God.*

(Galatians 5:18-21 EDNT)

Fruit of the Spirit

*22. But **the fruit of the Spirit is love, and love brings joy, peace, longsuffering, gentleness, goodness, faith, 23. tolerance and self-control: and no law exists against any of these.** 24. And those who belong to Christ have nailed the flesh to the cross with its passions and appetites. 25. **Since we live in the Spirit, we should be guided by the Spirit in our orderly walk**. 26. Let us not have excessive pride or boastfulness about personal abilities, infuriating one another or causing others to be envious. (Galatians 5:22-26 EDNT)*

Leaders must correct the inferior,
before they can construct a superior.
A congregation cannot build on the ashes
of immorality or grow with only spectators.
There must be believers with a missional
lifestyle committed to making disciples.

Appendix F

How and Why Pristine Congregations Grew

A starting place was to create community and family faith-based education house to house. This was a teaching and learning process that reflects an open-door access to New Testament converts and new disciples. When the "how" is known, the antecedent reason or "why" the pristine faith-based congregations grew will be understood. To learn the antecedent "why" one must understand the "how" by engaging the interrogatives: who, when, what, where, how many, how long, etc.

How did the early faith-based movement, known as The Way, survive and grow in a multicultural society? How did a faith rooted deeply in Judaism maintain reliability and consistency confronted with the cross-cultural issues of those following Jesus? What were the antecedent causes for growth during the first 100 years when the pristine movement had few leaders and almost no structure? Why and how did their faith-based gatherings grow within the Greco-Roman culture with the only building for worship was a Jewish Temple? How did they proceed with their daily meetings going from house to house teaching and preaching despite opposition? How were communications handled between Hebrew, Greek and Latin?

The Jewish people concentrating on Hebrew and Latin and Greek were both official languages of the Roman Empire (with Latin remaining the one for the upper class). Yet a few strong leaders, Paul being a good example, were well acquainted with the languages used in the First Century. This gave the movement an open door to cross-cultural communication.

The ability to read, write, and speak multiple languages was a foundation for development. Knowing the foundation stones of Judaism and the essential elements of the Greco-Roman culture were a major asset in the New Testament era. Greek philosophic knowledge and the infrastructure of Roman roads, governmental and military presence together with a structured water supply systems opened trade and personal interaction among people during the early time of Christian influence. In the first two chapters of Luke's church history in Acts, one finds at least seven reasons for early New Testament growth.

1. **Assurance of Spiritual Promises:** The people were assured through divine promises (Holy Spirit and Christ's Return) (Acts 1:8-11)
2. **Acceptance of Outreach Strategy:** The people accepted a divine program (witness to the death in Jerusalem, Judaea, Samaria, and Uttermost). (Acts 1:8)
3. **Anointed with Divine Power:** The people were equipped with divine Power for evangelism. (Acts 1:8)
4. **Accountable to a Divine Person:** The people were accountable to a divine Person. "This same Jesus" would return and they would give an account of their work. (Acts 1:11)
5. **Acceptance of Chosen Leadership:** The people accepted divinely chosen personnel (Apostles, 70, etc.) (Acts 1:21-26)

6. **Active in Proclaiming Truth:** The people were active in proclamation. (Peter's Sermons and the Witnesses) (Acts 2:14-24)
7. **Advanced by Sharing Common Ground:** The people agreed in prayer and sharing. (All things common, one mind, etc.) (Acts 2:44-47)

A Baker's Dozen of Door Openers to the Community

<u>**To grow a relational congregation leadership must**</u>:

1. *Accentuate commonalties because differences divide while those things which are common unite a group.*
2. *Associate with local culture because no one should have to change their language, culture or place of residence just to hear the saving message of grace. Christianity did not begin with a single culture or ethnic group, but brought people together into a common lifestyle.*
3. *Stress quality instead of quantity because it is the quality of behavior rather than the numbers that count with God.*
4. *Concentrate on building people rather than buildings because it the people for whom Christ died and rose again.*
5. *Develop a broad-based inclusive culture which makes everyone feel comfortable.*
6. *Produce a relational theology that is practical and true to the nature of God and follows basic tenants of sacred scripture.*
7. *Stand on moral principles rather than political correctness.*

8. ***Honor*** *the people's moral heritage rather than cutting them off from family and friends because salvation should separate one from their sins not their friends.*

9. ***Augment*** *the value of family and faith as a "value added" essential.*

10. ***Espouse*** *substance and the essence of moral truth rather than structure which attempts to arrange relations \between the parts.*

11. ***Emphasize*** *parenting, mentoring, and coaching for the young.*

12. ***Develop*** *a missional lifestyle that facilitates "as you go" into the world "make disciples."*

13. ***Draw*** *the community and churchgoers into a teaching/learning encounter within a "learning centered" approach to faith-based education which normally has a structured curriculum and provides student selection of classes/topics for study.*

Present Formal and Informal Aspects of Growth

The first Christian buildings to house the early operations were not constructed for at least 100 years after Pentecost. The Way was dependent on converted Jewish leaders and buildings and structures of Judaism and Rome, except for the homes of the people. The effect of organization and aging on the development is difficult to gasp; all that seems relevant to the present: as the buildings increased and the structure grew the outreach and growth declined. Gradually, the church became a "building" or a place instead of people. This greatly influenced development and still hinders the out-reach and evangelism of present day faith-based efforts. As the structure development and the permanent buildings were constructed more and different individuals gained influence on the people. This shaped what we now call "church."

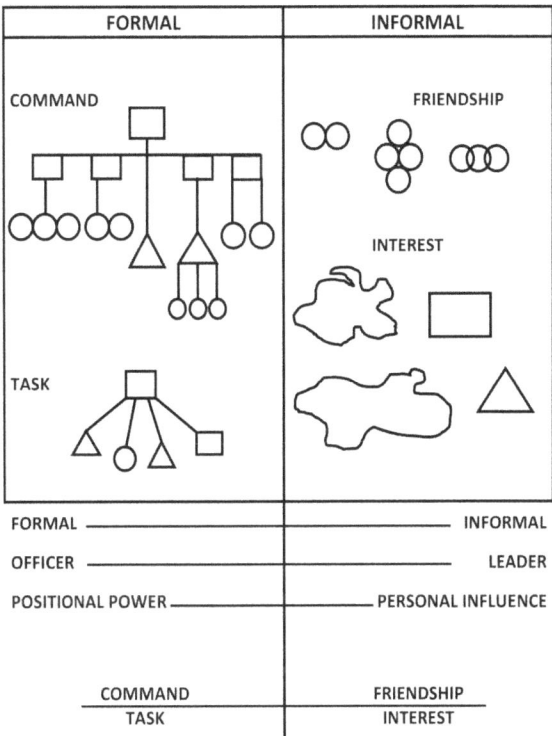

Positional and Personal Influence

It is vital that leaders understand the basic difference in positional and personal influence. The Command and Task structure is on the formal side and is designed to maintain *status quo*. This structure provides stability and continuity for an organization. This is where the organizational tree can be seen. Outreach, growth and extension comes from the informal aspects of the operation: friendship and interest. Individuals are attracted because of interest and attached because of friendship and fellowship. Evangelism, outreach, and true spiritual influence always comes from individuals on the informal operations of the organization. On the formal side are the officers with positional authority; on the informal side are the leaders with personal influence. The teaching ministry of the congregation is structured on the formal side; however, individuals are attracted to subjects and study classes by the teacher their ability to transfer "content" to the learner. They are retained by the quality of the teaching. A class structure is vertical and does not depend on friends or fellowship.

Arbitrary assigning individuals to classes by age, or gender does not work; individuals need a choice. My memory of a nephew who moved from Tennessee to Florida and following his mother's guidance found a church near his home. The first Sunday, he, his wife and small son went to the church "around the corner" they were met in the vestibule by a welcome committee who divided by age and gender. One took the boy of down the hall, another took the wife to a class and the husband to another. After the classes the husband and wife found each other in the sanctuary, but the boy was not present. Troubled they asked where the children are. The answer disturbed them greatly, *"They have an extended service especially for children."* There was no attention given to the worship only uneasiness about their son. After the worship service the couple went back to the vestibule and the same lady brought the young boy to them. Upon his return, the boy said *"Daddy, I don't wike it, I just don't wike it!"* The father responded, *"Your mother and I don't wike it either....and we won't be back."* This event discouraged the family from finding a church home. You can probably figure out the rest of the story. It was not good!

Present Day Input-Output-Feedback Model of Congregational Growth

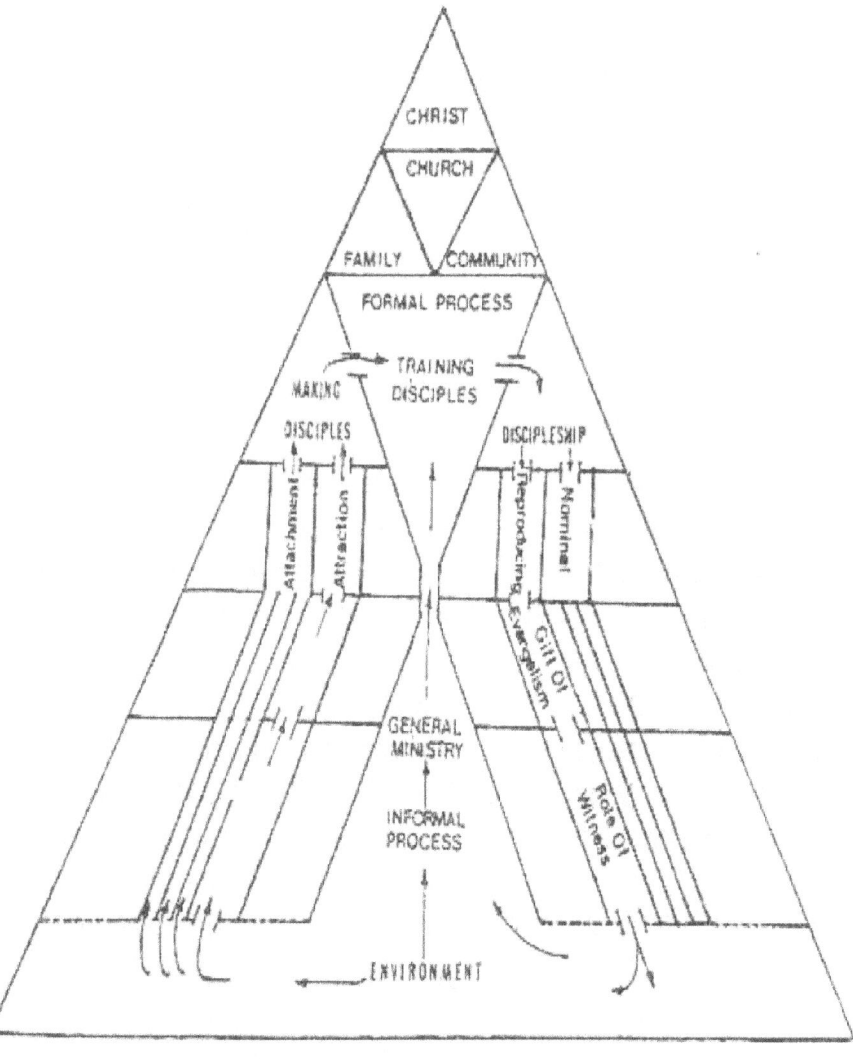

The Figure following shows the present process in the formal and informal aspects of Congregational development. The **formal process** of ministry at the local level is **training disciples**; while the **general ministry** is an **informal process** that flows to the **environment** and larger community where the place of worship is located. The young disciples move into the **formal training program** of the congregation and are sent into the community as witnesses. Some go as **nominal disciples** (in name only) and do nothing, others become **reproducing disciples** using their spiritual gifts for evangelism and maintain an active lifestyle witness to the general public. As they move through the maturing process they infiltrate the environment and plant the seeds of salvation in good ground. This feeds the soul-winning outreach and moves converts by **attraction** and **attachment** into the **disciple making** process.

Where is your "place" of Service?

In Genesis the concept of knowing one's place is taught in the life of Joseph. He claimed his place in the Promised Land. (Genesis 50: 24-26) The Bible teaches the Blessing of Abraham's Seeds (Galatians. 3:7f). Acts teaches that God gave particular territory to individuals and groups. (Acts 17:26). Some made a territorial commitment and claimed their community. (2 Corinthians 10:13-16) Assigned territory was given priority. Present day Christians sometimes leap frog over their family and community needs to foreign missions. To find your place listen to the Spirit!

Steps to Opening a Community

Open Heavens, Hearts, Homes, Hands, Highways

For where your treasure is, there your heart will be also. (Luke 10:34)

Open Heavens

The best way to open the windows of heaven is to financially support kingdom efforts to advance the gospel. This is a proven plan to produce the funds to expand the message of grace to the community. (Malachi 3:8-12)

Open Hearts

45. A good man produces a good treasure from his heart; and an evil man produces plunder that is evil: for from the abundance of the heart the mouth speaks. (Luke 6:45 EDNT)

20. And these are they who received the word on good ground; such as hear the word, and receives it, and becomes productive, some thirtyfold, some sixty, and some an hundredfold. (Mark 3:20 EDNT)

Open Homes

46. And they agreed to meet daily in the temple and to break bread from house to house, and they took meals cheerfully and with personal commitment. 47. Praising God and having favor with all the people. And the Lord added to the church daily those being saved. (Acts 2:46-47 EDNT)

Open Hands

I desire therefore the men to pray in every place lifting up holy hands with no anger in their hearts and no doubts in their minds. (1 Timothy 2:8 EDNT)

Open Highways

12. So, then, lift up the drooping hands, and the weak knees; 13. and plant your feet in a straight path, lest someone who is weak stumble out of the path; but be restored to strength instead. (Hebrews 12:12-13 EDNT)

DEACON TAKE A WALK

26. A messenger of the Lord spoke to Philip, saying, <u>Arise and go along the desert road from Jerusalem to Gaza.</u> 27. So he went on his journey and saw a man of Ethiopia, an Eunuch of the Court of Candace Queen of the Ethiopians, who had charge of her treasure and had come to Jerusalem to worship, 28. and was returning and was sitting in his chariot reading the Prophet Isaiah. 29. The Spirit spoke to Philip, <u>Go near and join yourself to this chariot.</u> 30. And Philip ran and heard him read the Prophet Isaiah, and said, <u>Can you understand what you are reading?</u> 31. And he said, <u>How can I, except someone guide me?</u> And he invited Philip to come up and sit with him. 32. The portion of scripture which he was reading was, As a sheep led to the slaughter and as a lamb before the shearer is silent, so He opened not His mouth: 33. In His humiliation He was denied justice: and who shall declare their wickedness? For His life is taken from the earth. 34. And the eunuch said to Philip, <u>Tell me about whom the prophet is speaking, of Himself or of another?</u> 35. Then Philip began at the same scripture and told him the good news about Jesus.

(Acts 8:26-35 EDNT)

Bibliography And Reading List

Allen, Bem P. (12002) Personality Theories: Development, Growth, American Psychoanalytic Association, 49(1). 187-215.

Applegate, J. & Shapiro, J. (2005). Neurobiology for Clinical Social approach to adoption support. Adoption & Fostering, 28(4).

Archer, C., & Gordon, C. (2004). *Parent mentoring*: an innovative

Barkley, (Eds.) *Child psychopathology* (2nd ed.)(pp. 632-684). Bass.

Beals, Arthur L. (2001). *When the Saints Go Marching Out! Mobilizing the Church for Mission.* Louisville: Geneva Press.

Bernstein, V., Harris, E., Long, C., Iida, E., & Hans, S. (2005). Issues Biological and psychological consequences, 13(3), 473-489. Biological influences on development. Developmental Review, birth of the human infant. Psychoanalytic Study of the Child, 28.

Comer, J. P.(2002). *Waiting for a Miracle*: Why Schools Can't Solve conception to adolescence. Malden, MA: Blackwell Publishing.

Conn, Harvie, Med. (1996). *Planting and Growing Urban Churches: From Dream to Reality.* Grand Rapids, MI: Baker Book House

Dale, Felicity. (2003). *Getting Started: A Practical Guide to House Church Planting.* Karis Publishing, Inc.

Dollar, Harold. (1996). *St. Luke's Missiology: A Cross-cultural Challenge.* Pasadena: William Carey Library.

Green, Hollis L. (2007). *Why Churches Die.* Nashville: geaPress.

Green, Hollis L. *(*2010). *Discipleship.* Nashville: geaPress.

Green, Hollis L. (*2010). Sympathetic Leadership Cybernetics.* Nashville: geaPress.

Green, Hollis L. *(*2010). *Why Christianity Fails in America*. Nashville: geaPress..

Green, Hollis L. *(2012). Titanic Lessons.* Nashville: geaPress.

Green, Hollis L. *(2012). Why Wait Till Sunday?* Nashville: geaPress..

Green, Hollis L. *(2013). Fighting the Amalekites.* Nashville: geaPress.

Green, Hollis L. *(2013). Tear Down These Walls.* Nashville: geaPress.

Green, Hollis L. (2013). *Remedial and Surrogate Parenting.* Nashville;geaPress

Green, Hollis L. *(2015, 2018). The EVERGREEN Devotional New Testament – C.A.F.E. Edition*. Nashville: geaPress.

Green, Hollis L. *(*2018). *The Children's Bread.* Nashville: geaPress.

Griffith, Jim and Bill Easum. (2008). *Ten Most Common Mistakes Made by Church Starts.* Chalice Press.

Herron, Fred. (2003). *Expanding God's Kingdom through Church Planting*. Lincoln, NE: iUniverse.

Johnson, M., & Karmiloff-Smith, A.(2004). *Neuroscience*

Journal of Social Psychology, 140(3). 357-365.

Moore, Ralph. (2002). *Starting a New Church: The Church Planter's Guide to Success.* Ventura, CA: Regal Books.

Payne, J.D. (2007).*Missional House Churches: Reaching Our Communities with the Gospel*. Colorado Springs, CO: Paternoster.

Rainey, Joel. (2008). *Planting Churches in the Real World.* Missional Press.

Reid, Alvin. (2009). *Evangelism Handbook: biblical, Spiritual, Intentional, Missional.* Nashville, TN: Broadman & Holman.

Roberts, Bob Jr. (2006). *Transformation: How Glocal Churches Transform Lives and the World.* Grand Rapids: Zondervan Publishing CO.

Roberts, Jr, Bob. (2008). *The Multiplying Church: The New Math for Starting New Churches.* Grand Rapids, MI: Zondervan,

Schore, A.N. (2003). Affect Regulation and Repair of the Self. New Sciences, 96 (3). 871-875.

Searcy, Nelson and Kerick Thomas. (2007), *Launch: Starting a New Church from Scratch.* Regal Books.

Smith, Steven. (2013). *The Key to Deep Change: Experiencing Spiritual Transformation by Facing Unfinished Business.* Lakeland, FL: Creative Equippers,.

Solms, M. & Turnbull, O. (2002). The Brain and the Inner World: Special issue on forensic developmental psychology,22(3).

Stetzer, Edward J. (2006) *Planting Missional Churches.* Nashville, TN: B&H Publishers

Van Engen, Charles E. (1991). *God's Missionary People: Rethinking the Purpose of the Local Church.* Grand Rapids: Baker Book House.

www.ingramcontent.com/pod-product-compliance
Lightning Source LLC
Chambersburg PA
CBHW070736170426

43200CB00007B/536